Freedom to Play

We Made Our Own Fun

Studies in Childhood and Family in Canada

Studies in Childhood and Family in Canada is a multidisciplinary series devoted to new perspectives on these subjects as they evolve. The series features studies that focus on the intersections of age, class, race, gender, and region as they contribute to a Canadian understanding of childhood and family, both historically and currently.

Series Editor
Cynthia Comacchio
Department of History
Wilfrid Laurier University

Manuscripts to be sent to
Brian Henderson, Director
Wilfrid Laurier University Press
75 University Avenue West
Waterloo, Ontario, Canada, N2L 3C5

Freedom to Play

We Made Our Own Fun

NORAH L. LEWIS, EDITOR

Studies in Childhood and Family in Canada

Wilfrid Laurier University Press

WLU

This book has been published with the help of a grant from the Humanities and Social Sciences Federation of Canada, using funds provided by the Social Sciences and Humanities Research Council of Canada. We acknowledge the financial support of the Government of Canada through the Book Publishing Industry Development Program for our publishing activities.

National Library of Canada Cataloguing in Publication Data

Freedom to play : we made our own fun / Norah L. Lewis, editor.

(Studies in childhood and family in Canada series)
Includes bibliographical references.
ISBN 0-88920-406-3

1. Amusements—Canada—History—20th century.   I. Lewis, Norah Lillian, 1935-   II. Series.

GV1204.15.F74 2002   790.1'922'0971'0904   C2002-903296-2

© 2002 Wilfrid Laurier University Press
Waterloo, Ontario, Canada N2L 3C5
www.wlupress.wlu.ca

Cover design by Kathy Joslin.
Cover photograph: All sails set, undated (Kelowna Museum and Archives).

Every reasonable effort has been made to acquire permission for copyright material used in this text, and to acknowledge all such indebtedness accurately. Any errors and omissions called to the publisher's attention will be corrected in future printings.

Printed in Canada

In loving memory of, and in gratitude to,
Mac and Mrs. Mac
(Henry and Jean McAughey)

CONTENTS

PLAYING IS PLAYING WHEN SHARED

PLAYING IS PLAYING GAMES

THERE WAS ALWAYS SOMETHING TO DO

LIST OF ILLUSTRATIONS

ACKNOWLEDGMENTS

I am grateful to Neil Sutherland and Jean Barman for their encouragement and wise advice, Joyce McLean for her careful reading of the manuscript and my long-suffering and indulgent husband who served as critic and proofreader. I greatly appreciate those who contributed to this project either through interviews, conversations or written contributions: Don Clay, Eileen Scott Campbell, Harold Zwick, R.B. Green, Earl Sherman, Peggy Sherman, Rolland Lewis, Dick Saunders, Judy Wells, Paul Barker, Kim Hilliard, Tony Plomp, Ann Rogers, Ivy Moulton, Dawn McKim, Bill Wells, Janet Reid, Janet Marshall, Jean Wilson, Henry Barone, Ina Trudgeon, Freda Mallory, Margaret Walker, Fred Greaves, Hugh and Jim McCullum, Margaret Nichols, Lis Schmidt Robert, Helen Hansen, Laurena Saunders, Ken Strong, Marilyn Barker, Glen Sullivan, Ian and Lee Rennie, Norman St. Clair-Sulis, W.J. Phillips, Nick Green, and Donna Ebbutt. I also thank my extended family and many friends who discussed this topic with me and shared their memories.

I am grateful to librarians at Richmond Public Library and University of British Columbia Library for their help in securing materials through interlibrary loan. And of course to Dr. Brian Henderson, Elin Edwards, Carroll Klein, and former director Sandra Woolfrey of Wilfrid Laurier University Press for their encouragement and direction.

I also appreciate the generosity of friends and of the following archives for providing photographs: Archives of the Anglican Diocese of New Westminster, British Columbia Provincial

Archives, Vancouver Public Library Special Collections, National Archives of Canada, Saskatchewan Archives Board, Public Archives of Prince Edward Island, Kelowna Museum Archives, Provincial Archives of Newfoundland and Labrador, and Prince Rupert City and Regional Archives.

Section-Opening Photographs

Go Outside and Play: found photograph, provided by Norah Lewis.

Playing Is Playing When Shared: prairie children's party c. 1900. Courtesy of Vera Hoknes.

Playing Is Playing Games: photo of Keith and Kim Gosse, 1952. Farm near Nechako River. Photo courtesy of Evelyn Gosse.

Creating Their Own Equipment: Ian McLetchie with Margaret McLetchie Nichols at Magog, Quebec, 1944. Photo courtesy of Margaret Nichols.

Animals: Friend, Foe, or Food: boy with goat. Photo courtesy of the Vancouver Public Library [4845].

There Was Always Something to Do: everyone absorbed in catching crabs. Behind Ivory Island Lighthouse. Kim and Cindy Gosse and the lighthouse keepers' children, 1951. Photo courtesy of Evelyn Gosse.

INTRODUCTION

*My most pleasant memory of childhood is the absolute free-
dom we had. Absolute freedom! We could do anything we
liked. We weren't destructive, but we could just roam all
over the country. It was ours to look at and enjoy. There was
so much to see and do. We never had time hanging on our
hands, not one bit.*
— *Don Clay, recalling his 1920s childhood*

Play, wrote Friedrich Froebel, founder of the kindergarten movement, is the highest phase of child development and the purest,
most spiritual activity of young children.[1] Through play, children test the rules of cause and effect, utilize deductive and
inductive reasoning, and develop their imaginative and creative
thinking skills.[2] They also experience strength in cooperation,
challenge in competition, and satisfaction and pleasure in alone-
ness. Kinesiologist Glynn A. Leyshon believes play helps children build optimism and hope in their lives. Neil Sutherland, a
historian of Canadian childhood, considers play the most important experience in the culture of childhood. Learning to function
in their own milieu helps children prepare for the adult world
they will enter.[3]

This study attempts to view those games, activities, and
amusements that were part of the culture of Canadian childhood
from 1900 to the mid-1950s, the years before television became
standard equipment in most homes. The sources used include:
letters written to the children's pages of five weekly rural news-

papers; written contributions or interviews with thirty-nine people and short conversations with many others; and selections taken from the writing of nine Canadian authors.

As Camilla Gryski observes in *Let's Play: Traditional Games of Childhood*, children have been playing the same games, with local variations, for a very long time. Pieter Brueghel's painting *Children's Games* (1559) includes many games that chidren still play. British folklorists Iona and Peter Opie concluded in their study *Lore and Language of Schoolchildren*, that the culture of childhood is kept alive through games, rhymes, chants, riddles, catcalls, and retorts that children learn orally and pass on to others. Soeur Marie Ursula's study of the Lavalois family of Quebec also confirms that traditional games, songs, and stories are part both of family lore and family practice. D.N. Panabaker recalled that among large Pennsylvania Dutch families in Waterloo, Ontario, adults often participated with children in the same games and pastimes.[4] American historian Elliott West concluded that children moving to the western frontier brought with them "the rich lore of childhood — rhymes, word puzzles, songs jokes and games."[5] This lore and skill enabled newcomers to connect and build rapport with other children in spite of language and ethnic differences, although the content of some folk rhymes and songs may have perpetuated negative attitudes toward specific ethnic groups or social classes.

Elderly Canadians recall, and historians and educators confirm, that playtime and playthings for today's children differ from those of their own generation. They could, they recall, store all their toys in one apple box or in the bottom drawer of the kitchen cabinet. Life and pleasures, they feel, were simpler, and many believe that as children they had more fun than today's children have. A walk through the local toy store reveals that many of the games they used are still available, although Lego for example, has replaced Meccano as a popular building set. Running, jumping, pushing, pulling, rolling, climbing, circling, and emulating the occupations and activities of adults, however, are still the basis for many play activities.[6]

From another perspective, today's youngsters are surprised to learn that the elderly were once young: Grandfather was marble champion of his school; Grandmother skipped Double Dutch to two hundred; Great-Aunt Eileen trapped rabbits during wartime and sold the pelts to line airmen's helmets; Great-Uncle Earl shot his first Canada goose at age eleven. When questioned about the fun they had, these "ancient ones" respond with faraway looks in their eyes and slight smiles on their faces, and then relate the games they played and the fun they had. At some point they utter the inevitable phrase, "In those days we made our own fun!"

The Players

The players in this study were Canadian and Newfoundland children. (Newfoundland became a province of Canada in 1949.) A record of children's activities is contained in hundreds of letters written to the children's pages of five newspapers that catered to rural interests and concerns. When children wrote to the Pathfinders Club — *Free Press Prairie Farmer*; Maple Leaf Club — *Family Herald and Weekly Star*; The Beaver Circle — *The Farmer's Advocate*; Young Canada Club — *Grain Growers' Guide*; and Young Co-operators — *The Western Producer*, they automatically became club members, and hoped their letters would be printed on the children's page. Letter writers ranged in age from five to sixteen years for most clubs, although both the *Family Herald and Weekly Star* and *The Western Producer* included sections for writers from seventeen to nineteen.[7]

Children wrote to tell fellow readers about their daily lives and the events they witnessed that are now part of Canadian history. Each letter is the written record of one child at a specific time in the life of that child, and deals with play, games, or amusements. Letters writers were a select although diverse group, literate in English, motivated to write, and mostly rural.

A number of individuals were asked to reflect on their memories of childhood games and activities. They, too, represented a diversity of childhoods including both single-child and multi-child, working-class and middle-class families from diverse cultural and geographic backgrounds. Most provided written accounts, although seven contributors were interviewed.

Three individuals who initially agreed to contribute found recalling their childhoods so painful that they withdrew their offers. This was a reminder that not all childhoods were happy, nor does time necessarily ease pain. Many others contributed memories during casual conversations when the subject of play was raised. The third source is selections taken from the writings of eleven Canadian writers who described specific games or activities in their own childhoods or, in some cases, the activities of other children.

Just chatting. Barnett area of the Fraser Valley, 1907 (Vancouver Public Library, Special Collections [7686]).

There are, of course, problems in reconstructing the past through adult memories. First, memories can be faulty as they can be coloured by time, subsequent experiences, and frequent retelling. Second, individuals tend to be selective in which memories they retain. Contributors tended to focus on idyllic childhoods filled with pleasant events and happy times, the kind of childhoods we pretend are normal for all children. Although this collection does not reflect the darkest of children's experiences, it does provide a window into the world of children's games and activities of fifty to a hundred years ago.

Elliott West suggests three standards that minimize the bias of materials used in this book. First, the more clear and exact the memory, the more likely it is to be accurate. Second, repetition of the same memory from many different persons lends credence. Third, congruence lends credibility when reminiscences correspond with those of other sources. Taken together the sources reveal that play was very much a part of the culture of childhood, and that the sources used provide a reliable record.[8] Further support for the use of such materials is given by Australian historians Gwyn Dow and June Factor who, in their book *Australian Childhood: An Anthology,* demonstrate how clearly the previously unheard voices of historical children can be heard through the judicious selection of a variety of sources and resources.[9]

Go Outside and Play

When children completed their work, or parents and teachers tired of their noise, they were ordered to "Go outside and play." And children fled, hoping that out of sight was out of mind. Girls probably had less free time than boys, as they helped with never-ending housework and child-minding.[10] Few girls wanted a small child tagging along, but siblings were important playmates and many families, including parents, played games together.[11]

But as both memories and research indicate, not all children found or were allowed time to play. The family economic situation may have required that children help about the home or find a paying job outside the home. Children were a cheap and readily accessible source of labour. At the age of fourteen, Ben Powell, from Carboneau, Newfoundland, worked a man's job to help support his parents and eight siblings; at age nine, Chinese-Canadian Sing Lim worked for a farmer, thirteen hours a day, six days a week, during the summer months.[12]

In other cases, parents, guardians, or employers were determined to control every moment and movement of children's lives. In a letter dated January 13, 1904, to the Maple Leaf Club of the *Family Herald and Weekly Star,* a young Ontario boy wrote to tell of the appalling abuse suffered by a little English orphan who had been placed with a local farmer by a Children's Home.[13] Sing Lim described the ill-treatment of a young Chinese-Canadian boy by the child's guardian, and a survivor of the pioneer era reported to Barry Broadfoot that when he was about six years old he put away his toys, slingshot, and pets because work took precedence over play.[14] In other families, religious teachings or cultural attitudes deemed play as frivolous if not sinful; time was not to be wasted on such foolishness.

Many children ranged far and wide as they explored their world, alone, with their dogs, or with other children. Jacqueline Bliss concluded that "Girls appear to lead an unrestricted life on the prairies, working and playing hard." Eliza Eby and her brother roamed the prairie, picking berries, digging Indian turnips (Jack-in-the pulpit), and fishing.[15] An elderly Alberta woman observed that to her the open land opened up the possibilities of running wildly, freely, and seemingly endlessly.[16] And in recalling his Alberta childhood, physician Charles MacKenzie said, "We roamed everywhere, we explored the creek, we found birds' nests, coyote burrows, and even a bob cat up a tree."[17] The Daleys' Prince Edward Island farm bordered Fullerton Marsh where it emptied into the Hillsborough River. The Daley children swam, rowed, and played in the marsh.[18] The Clay boys grew up in and around Victoria, with two years at Ocean Falls. Don Clay recalls, "We could roam all over the country. It was ours to look at and enjoy. There was so much to see and do."[19]

At the same time, urban children were playing on streets and sidewalks, in back alleys, city parks, vacant lots, undeveloped woodlands, and along creeks and river banks. In 1911, James Gray's family moved to Winnipeg, a "lusty, gutsy, frontier boom-town."[20] Gray and his friends turned vacant lots into baseball diamonds or snow-packed hockey rinks, or played cops and robbers among abandoned houses. Bicycles extended their range to distant parts of the city and into the surrounding countryside.

Ina Trudgeon recalls that for children, in Vancouver during the 1920s, the streets were their playground, and they moved aside only for cars. "Our parents never seemed to worry about us," she said.[21] Leyshon notes that in 1930s working-class areas of Hamilton, most children played "out on the pavement, in back alleys and in back lanes" until dark.[22] Lorraine Blashill found that most children of the 1950s felt safe within their communities although they were usually unsupervised.[23] On looking back, adults recalled that their feelings of independence and adventure were fuelled by their inquisitiveness and daring, and the release, if only for a short time, from the work, stress, and confinement of their daily lives.

The freedom of children living in detention camps during wartime and in Indian residential schools was restricted by fences, limited space, and the attitude of the surrounding community. Both Joy Kogawa and Shizuye Takashima remember that interned Japanese-Canadian children were physically and socially isolated from nearby communities, but they were usually free to explore their nearby environs. This was however, small compensation for being uprooted and interned.[24] First Nations children, accustomed to roaming and hunting in forests and fields, found residential school life confining, and many called the school "jail." Most residential schools, however, owned sizable pieces of property, and the boys' play area was often larger than the immediate school grounds.[25] Girls, on the other hand, were rarely granted the same degree of freedom as boys.[26]

Playing Is Playing When Shared

Children's play, particularly outdoor play, generally involved physical activities, was self-organized, required little or no equipment, and was executed with a great deal of noise.[27] As Gryski noted, although the details of traditional games have changed over time, the patterns remain the same. "We still love to jump and hop, throw and catch, chase and hide."[28] Canadian folklorist Edith Fowke lists fifteen categories of games played by children in her collection *Red Rover, Red Rover: Children's Games Played in Canada*, eight of which included chasing, catching, seeking, hunting, racing, duelling, exerting, or daring.[29]

Gray noted that players decided what to play, rarely played a game to completion, and played the same games again and again.[30] Ina Trudgeon recalls: "We just picked up any old thing like a can, and we played a game until we got tired of it and then we'd go on to something else."[31] Youngsters also emulated the activities, occupations, characteristics, attitudes, and actions of adults from their traditional cultures, specific occupations, and, of course, their teachers.

Children had their favourite games, but what they played was often determined by the season of the year, equipment and number of players available, or which child was the bossiest. With the first snowfall, children tramped out the wheel-and-spoke pattern for Fox and Goose. Games such as Mother May I?, Red Light, or Hoist Your Sails required no equipment, but certainly generated a lot of action and noise.

A tea party, with Adele, Florence, and Marion Newberry, undated (Prince Edward Island Public Archives and Records Office [3885/66]).

Other games required simple bits of equipment—a rope to skip, a small flat stone or a piece of coloured glass as a toss for hopscotch, a ball that would bounce for "One, Two, Three, O'Leary," Ordinary Moving, or Ante-I-Over, and a tin can for Kick the Can. Bernadette Yuan and her friends put a ball in the toe of a woman's stocking. They then swung the stocking, first with one hand and then with the other, in a sequence of moves to hit various parts of the body in a specific order.[32] Girls who skipped the intricate steps of China (or Chinese) skip sometimes made their skipping ropes of elastic bands linked together.

Action games generally required spaced, but Leyshon noted that children, living in the working-class area of Hamilton during the 1930s, simply adapted their traditional games to fit the limited spaces of streets and alleys.[33]

Playing Is Playing Games

It was a sure sign of spring in a rural school when the school board purchased a new softball and, sometimes, a new bat. Evelyn Slater

McLeod recalled that in the early 1900s the children at her school used a ball of twine with a canvas cover and a bat that was just a stick of wood. Ball was the favourite spring and summer sport, and a game against another school or team was a special event. Arline Huminuk recalls the excitement at her rural Manitoba school when players arrived from a neighbouring school for a softball or hockey game.[34]

Urban school boards also provided only minimal equipment—usually a ball and bat for each diamond on the school grounds. Neil Sutherland and Fred Greaves remember pitching competitions held throughout Vancouver schools. A plywood box with a hole at the level of a good pitch was placed on home plate. Players, primarily boys, attempted to throw the ball through the hole. As there were awards for the best pitchers, youngsters set up similar boxes in their backyards in order to practise their pitching skills. The award was a ticket to a ball game at Nat Bailey Stadium.[35]

Winter meant snow forts and snowball fights, snow angels and tunnels, dug through snowbanks that provided escapes from invading forces. Even small hills seemed high to young children who felt they could slide forever on sleds, toboggans, cardboard, tea trays, or barrel-stave skis. Girls, often in ill-fitting skates and bundled in layers of clothing, became Sonja Henie or Barbara Ann Scott. Boys, in mismatched outfits with little or no padding, knew they were potential hockey greats in the mold of Maurice Richard or Syl Apps. The Buchanan boys played hockey with curved willow branches and an unlimited supply of "pucks" (road apples). Ted Logie and his Okanagan friends played knobbies, a make-believe form of lacrosse, with sticks cut from a nearby bush.[36] As basic as their equipment was, players had fun.

Hockey was the primary winter sport. Rinks were flooded in schoolyards, backyards, and parks. Where there was no ice, children played on packed snow, grass, or streets. As youngsters outgrew their ice skates and other equipment, they traded it around or passed it on to another child. It seemed as though no one ever got new skates.[37]

Except for goal pads, hockey players usually supplied their own equipment. During the 1930s, Frank Sullivan made goal and shin pads for young players by stitching willow sticks into legs torn from old denim overalls that were then sewn to the tops of old felt socks. The pads were held in place by rubber bands cut from old inner tubes. Henry Barone and his Toronto teammates made shin pads by stuffing magazines down the front of their socks and shoulder pads from thick layers of newspapers. Only league teams wore matching sweaters, and these were often supplied by local service clubs, commercial outlets, or benevolent associations.[38] As former hockey player Ken Dryden noted, participation in minor hockey leagues grew from less than 14,000 boys in 1930 to almost 100,000 players in 1957. Furthermore, more parents began taking their boys to the rink.[39]

Residential school girls and boys were all supplied with skates, but Basil Johnston recalls that it was the senior hockey team that got the most ice time and the best hockey sticks. All other players were allotted one stick for the season. Players went to great efforts to shape their sticks to suit themselves, and if the stick broke or cracked, owners repaired them with glue, tape, and tin.[40] Residential school teams were usually good players. Glen Tibbitts played with the Forwarren, Manitoba, hockey team in the same league as the Birtle, Manitoba, residential school team. "They [the Indian boys] were excellent players," Tibbitts recalls, "and the Foxwarren team enjoyed playing against them. In fact, some of them were so good that, when the boys left residential school, local teams recruited them to play in the Manitoba Intermediate League."[41] For First Nations players, sports was an outlet for their energy, an opportunity to display their skill as players, a time to form close friendships with other players, and a chance to get away from the school and out into the community.[42]

Although residential school girls were competent softball and basketball players, they usually did not play in local leagues. Kamloops Residential School, however, had a well-trained dance troupe that performed at community functions and jamborees. Not all dancers enjoyed practising or dancing in public, but dancing to the radio or to records was a favourite activity among girls of all ages.[43]

The line between what were deemed boys' activities and girls' activities was not clearly defined, but it was probably more acceptable for girls to be "tomboys" than for boys to be "sissies." Helen Porter noted that in the district of St. John's, Newfoundland, where she grew up, most games were played by both sexes, although girls were more adept at jacks and skipping than were boys.[44]

McDonough recalls that children enforced fair play and tolerance for younger, less skillful players.[45] But John Charyk reports that other people have different memories—such as the lone grade one child or the only girl in the small school who were ignored or rejected by the boys.[46] For some children rejection was culturally, racially, or socially based. When Fredelle Bruser Maynard entered school in Winnipeg, she met overt prejudice against Jews. Sing Lim and his Vancouver Chinatown friends walked home in groups as protection against local bullies.[47]

There were, of course, times and games when competition was keen. Marble playing usually heralded the arrival of spring, except in Montreal and McGregor, Manitoba, where youngsters played marbles year round. With practice, players became highly skillful with bolo bats and yoyos. Sidewalk and street-corner demonstrations and competitions (sponsored by the Cheerio Yoyo Company) taught children a range of moves and patterns that players could do. Prizes such as yoyo strings or a new yoyo or bolo bat were offered to the winners. Fred Greaves recalls yoyos in three colours for three different prices: red and white at 25 cents; black at 35 to 50 cents; and gold at 50 to 75 cents.[48]

Creating Their Own Equipment

Manufactured toys and equipment were constant sources of interest. Youngsters pored over the Eaton's and Simpson's Christmas catalogues, for therein they saw wonderful toys, games, and other equipment they hoped to own. Catalogue pictures provided patterns or models that inspired children to build, sew, or create similar toys.

Girls were expected to play with dolls, although some boys also had dolls. Bernice McDonough and her sisters made their rag dolls from old stockings or sweaters.[49] Seepeetza's mother sewed rag dolls on her sewing machine. Ruby Stonehouse wrote to say she had taken apart her rag doll to wash, dry, and iron her

before putting her back together.[50] The *Family Herald and Weekly
Star* not only provided a pattern and specific instructions for
making a rag doll but also offered a prize to the child who made
the best doll.[51] Manufactured dolls were more desirable and
more expensive than rag dolls, and envied, indeed, was the child
who received an Eaton's Beauty or a Shirley Temple doll as a
Christmas or birthday present.[52] Eileen Scott Campbell recalled
that her lovely dolls came from relatives in Britain. Gifts from
the old country or relatives working elsewhere generally
included treasures that the family could not afford or that were
not available in local stores. Each junior residential school girl
was given her own doll or teddy bear, and from bits of fabric or
pieces of yarn she often sewed or knitted clothes for her doll.
Others made little dolls of bark, cloth, and string.[53]

The Newham girls with their dolls, undated
(Saskatchewan Archives Board [R-A 19159]).

Building a winning soapbox racing car was the dream of
many boys and their fathers. Building them appears to have
been primarily a male activity. Fred Greaves and Bud Phillips
recall participants had a year to plan, construct, and paint their
racing machines. Less complicated, but probably no less fun,

were simple soapbox cars constructed from a piece of two-by-four with a box nailed on the top, roller skates for wheels, and a handle bar to hold.[54]

What children lacked in equipment they made up in ingenuity. Their imaginations could turn a discarded binder canvas (a slatted belt that carried the cut grain into the binder to be tied into sheaves) hung over a clothesline as a tent. A shady nook among the trees, a blanket spread on the grass, a few wooden boxes, a couple of cracked or broken dishes, and other discarded materials were used to play house, store, school, hospital, castle, or whatever children wanted to play on any particular day. And donning a few pieces of adult clothing set imaginations going as children assumed adult roles.[55]

Children also found many playthings in the world around them. The bladders of sea-wrack popped when walked on, kelp floats exploded when thrown on a fire, and blowguns could be made from the hollow stems of elderberries or cow parsnip. Dick Saunders and his friends "travelled" endless hours in the cab of an abandoned work train. Ivy and Jack Moulton's pony pulled the "arse cart" they constructed from various pieces of discarded farm implements.[56] Neil Bramble and his pals "drove" for miles, each holding a piece of board approximately six-by-twelve inches with a bent wire pulled through to simulate a speedometer. The boys provided appropriate vocal motor sounds. There was no end to what youngsters could create with what they found around them.[57]

Boys were more likely than girls to build tree houses, rafts, go-carts, soapbox cars, and sleds, and to make slingshots, bows and arrows, and wooden guns, but as Eileen Scott Campbell indicated, building rafts, sleds, and snow forts was not exclusively a male domain. Glen Sullivan and Dick Saunders both recall that their fathers taught and encouraged them in the use of basic tools. Smitty Glover's grandfather instructed him in the art of making a simple kite from two pieces of bamboo, old newspapers, paste, and string. One of Evelyn Slater McLeod's school mates made a pair of skis from barrel staves.[58] Leyshon provided both instructions and a diagram for making an elastic gun from a board, clothes pegs, and bands cut from an old inner tube.

Retired teacher Jack Dreidger provided detailed instructions for fashioning a slingshot, a popular implement for boys, from a Y-shaped willow branch, a scrap of good leather, elastic bands from an old inner tube, and string. He also described a merry-go-round built by the older students of Saskatchewan's Renfrew Rural School for use by the smaller students.[59]

If children ran out of ideas of things to do or make, the *Family Herald and Weekly Star, Free Press Prairie Farmer,* and other publications printed precise instructions for items as diverse as magic lanterns, skis, dollhouses, or sleds. There was no limit as to what a child could or would make.

Animals: Friend, Foe, or Food

What would youngsters have done without their pets to act as companions, playmates, consolers, and entertainers? Dogs accompanied youngsters on their rambles, and more than one youngster was saved from drowning, attack, or serious injury by a faithful dog. House cats were common. Laurena Saunders's Snooky allowed himself to be dressed in doll clothes and pushed about in a doll carriage.

Rural children made pets of lambs, calves, ducks, and other domestic animals, but farm animals were expected to contribute to the family economy as workers, part of the herd or flock, a marketable product, or food for the family larder. Many a youngster dissolved in tears as pet chickens or rabbits were prepared for a family dinner or shipped off to market, or the calf or pig he or she had trained, groomed, and shown at the farm club achievement day, was sold and led away, possibly to the slaughterhouse.

City bylaws notwithstanding, rabbits, chickens, geese, goats, and even horses and cows could commonly be found in back-yard pens and barns. Ina Trudgeon's father kept his teams of horses at the south end of the Cambie Bridge; her Great-Uncle George kept dairy cows near the south end of Oak Street until the early 1930s; and one of her young Vancouver neighbours owned a Shetland pony. She recalls that the pony was popular with local children, but the owner was not. Gary L. Saunders's Newfoundland pony, Beaver, served both as a pet and as the family workhorse.[60] The death of a beloved animal or bird was a traumatic experience, and children often marked the event with a funeral and burial.

Youngsters were also intrigued by and observant of wildlife. Their eyes and ears were attuned to sights and sounds of the world through the changing seasons. C. Howard Shillington recalled that the sight of wild geese flying in their V formation gave a special meaning to spring. Children often attempted to tame wild animals and birds, but only crows proved adaptable. With a bounty of two or three cents for crows' legs and eggs, they were more likely to be killed than tamed. But it was the ubiquitous gophers, who saw prairie grain fields and gardens as manna from heaven and theirs for the taking, that sharpened the hunting and trapping skills of many prairie youngsters. At a few cents a tail, gophers provided youngsters a source of income. Young hunters were encouraged by agronomists and political leaders, who believed gophers had the potential to destroy the economy of the West. The Saskatchewan Department of Agriculture designated May 1, 1917, as "gopher day." Children in the almost one thousand participating schools destroyed approximately a half million gophers that day.[61]

With hunting went guns, and guns were standard equipment, particularly in rural areas, to protect flocks and herds from predatory coyotes, foxes, and hawks seeking quick and easy dinners. Many youngsters owned their own guns or were permitted to use their parents' .22s or small-gauge shotguns. Journalist James Minifie recalled that his father gave him a .22 to hunt rabbits and birds. Ammunition was expensive and young hunters were soon expected to come back with a bird for every cartridge used.[62] D.H. Grigg recalled that young hunters of the early 1900s shot rabbits to feed the family.[63] As teenagers, Ruth Wray and her sisters supplemented their Nelson Island family income and food larder with grouse and deer they shot and fish they caught. At age ninety-five, Ruth's eyes still twinkled as she recalled the thrill of the hunt and her skill as a hunter.[64]

Hunting and trapping was a normal part of the traditional education of First Nations children. Basil Johnston's friend "Charlie Shoot" was so accurate with a slingshot he could hit a flying sparrow at fifty yards, graze a rabbit's ear at twenty-five paces, and get an apple from a tree by hitting the stem without touching the apple. One day he killed ten black squirrels which he then skinned, gutted, and cooked on a spit for lunch. Not every boy was as skillful as "Charlie Shoot."[65]

There Was Always Something to Do

Special days and holidays were welcome breaks from a routine of daily chores and seasonal tasks. Both Valentine's Day and Halloween were celebrated with classroom parties. The Halloween party gave youngsters an opportunity to wear masks, bob for apples, and play games.[66] In urban areas, children usually went door to door demanding "Halloween apples" or "trick or treat," and children were expected to do a trick for their treat. In rural areas, children were likely to visit only nearby neighbours. No one recalled being afraid that the treats were unsafe to eat, but they remembered which homes handed out the best homemade fudge or popcorn balls. A number of elderly adults laughed heartily as they related stories of outhouses they moved, gates they removed, fences they pushed over, chimneys they blocked, and farm machinery they hoisted onto barn or granary roofs—and how they did not get caught. It is possible that the magnitude of their escapades may have grown with the years.

The three biggest and most anticipated events of the school year were the annual school field day, the end-of-school picnic, and the Christmas concert. Typically all the schools in a given area met at a central point for competitions in elocution, music, track and field, and softball. There were ribbons for the winners of track-and-field events, and a banner or cup for the best ball team. In spite of little or no coaching and inadequate equipment, students practised for weeks to uphold the honour of their schools.

Everyone in the community stopped work and came to the end-of-school-year picnic. There were novelty races for children with prizes of five or ten cents, a ball game among the men of the community, and a picnic supper provided by the women. There was usually ice cream, either made on the spot in hand-cranked machines or brought in large padded cases from a nearby creamery. In some places the picnic was followed by a dance as there was certain to be someone among local residents who could play a fiddle or some other instrument.[67]

The third major community event of the school year was the Christmas concert. Teachers were expected to put on "good" concerts, and they were judged, in part, by the success of their students' performances. Students practised diligently and parents helped with costumes, sets, stages, and Christmas trees. Santa Claus always came. The concert was a magical time. Columnist Margaret Parker observed: "Have you ever transformed a very tangible little mortal into a fairy by the ruffly magic of crepe paper and tinsel? — or fitted the flowing cheesecloth robe and graceful wire-poised wings of an angel to the shoulders of an excited squirming young sinner?"[68]

John Charyk noted there was always a pageant or tableau and carols that reflected the religious significance of Christmas, although one mother expressed disgust that over the years her son's annual role was that of a shepherd. But no one cared if children forgot their lines or sang off key. "Not a single child was ever left out. No matter what his color, his nationality, his age, his size, or ability, every child was given equal opportunity to perform before an appropriate audience."[69]

Fredelle Bruser Maynard, the only Jewish girl in Birch Hills, Saskatchewan, participated in the annual Christmas concert with her schoolmates. Including her was undoubtedly meant as an act of kindness, but for Maynard the experience was a painful one.[70]

School boards usually paid for a present for each child, ordered through Eaton's Christmas Tree Shopping Service. A list, indicating the children's names, ages, and sex, was sent to Eaton's, and Eaton's provided a wrapped and labelled present for each child. Each child received a bag of candy and nuts, an apple, and sometimes an orange. During difficult economic times, these may have been the only Christmas presents some children received. Christmas concerts still provide happy memories for those who participated, teachers who prepared them, and those who watched.[71]

But Christmas could be a very lonely and difficult time for First Nations children who could not go home, and for Japanese-Canadian children held in detention camps. Basil Johnston recalls that those who remained at school tried to make the building seem less bleak and barren by bringing in cedar boughs and decorating the windows and walls.[72]

Christmas 1942, Takashima and her sister attended early morning Christmas services at the nearby Anglican Church. The community was not allowed to socialize with the Japanese Canadians from the camp, but several of the congregation wished the children "Merry Christmas," and the minister spoke with them. Later in the day their family ate Christmas dinner as cooked by father, played traditional Japanese music, and sang Japanese songs.[73] Sing Lim's family did not celebrate Christmas, but rather celebrated Chinese New Year, which for members of the Asian community, is a very special time.[74] Retaining family and cultural ties was essential and helped provide stability for the children.

Between 1900 and 1950, a growing number of groups, clubs, and societies for children and youth were sponsored by religious and cultural organizations and vocational institutions. The aims of such groups were quite specific—to ensure the proper spiritual, intellectual, moral, and physical development of the young, and to perpetuate traditional beliefs, cultural values, and mores. Letter writers described, and adults recalled, the good times and the comradeship of such groups.[75]

A significant number of rural children belonged to agricultural clubs sponsored and encouraged by university extension departments, provincial departments of agriculture, farmers' organizations, and agricultural newspapers. Such clubs were specifically aimed at encouraging young people to remain in rural areas and to train knowledgeable and competent future farm men and women.[76] Other letter writers and contributors indicated they were or had belonged to Girl Guides, Boy Scouts, Canadian Girls in Training (CGIT), Boys' Brigade, or other such organizations. Most former members indicated that they enjoyed the training, camping, and comradeship provided by such organizations and, in due time, encouraged their children to become members.

A more significant club in the eyes of many boys, was Cadets, supported and encouraged by the Strathcona Trust, and introduced in 1910 as formalized drill and military training in the physical education program in public schools. The aim of Cadets was to teach young men military obedience, precision, punctuality, manners, attentiveness to detail, self control, respect for age and authority, and willingness to defend their country. John Fedoruk, who joined Air Cadets in 1951, believes he learned the attributes listed above and, he added, Cadets helped him though his teens. Another former cadet, Bob Ogle, a priest and Member of Parliament, recalled that he loved everything about Cadets. Over the years, the membership of Cadets has waxed during wartime and waned during peacetime, and the program has changed and expanded to include naval and air cadets, and more recently, to include girls.[77] My young Chinese-Canadian neighbour, a recent immigrant from Hong Kong, loves Air Cadets. He not only enjoys the activities, but he has also found friends with whom he can relate.

The Junior Red Cross was initiated in 1914 as a means whereby children could support the war effort by raising money to assist Belgian orphans, contribute to the Patriotic Fund for the families of enlisted men, and pack parcels for soldiers. In 1919, the focus of the Junior Red Cross shifted to the promotion of good health, humanitarian ideals, good citizenship, and international friendship among children of the world. With the outbreak of war in 1939, Junior Red Cross members again did their bit for king and country, but they continued to promote good health care. Among other activities, boys and girls knit thousands of six-inch squares that were then sewn into afghans for use in military hospitals or for distribution to refugees. There is no doubt that Canadian and Newfoundland children made a major contribution to the war effort during both world wars by buying saving stamps, and collecting scrap metal and other materials.[78]

Organizations such as these taught reverence for God and respect for King, Empire, and Country, as well as for one another. Through the "League of the Empire" — An Imperial Union of Schools through Schools' and Pupils' Correspondence," children learned about the Motherland and the family of countries and colonies that made up the great British Empire. This concept of the great British Empire was reinforced through the school curricula in all provinces and by the Neilson Chocolate Company maps (Mercator's projection) in which the British Empire was shown in red. (Neilson provided free maps of the world and of Canada to Canadian classrooms.) Economist J. Stuart Prentice recalled that in 1901, he and his Manitoba classmates were "thoroughly British...and proud of the red blocs all over the maps of the world." Queen Victoria's birthday, May 24, was designated Empire Day and celebrated with parades, flags, patriotic readings, and the singing of "Rule Britannia," "The Red, White, and Blue," and "The Maple Leaf Forever."[79]

Patriotism was especially high during the war years. The public was bombarded with government propaganda that justified and reinforced the need for Canadians to go to war. Even children's games made a clear distinction between the "good guys" and the "bad guys." Joy Kogawa recalled a board game called "The Yellow Peril," marketed by Somerville Board Games, the aim of which was to defeat the Japanese.[80] Japanese-Canadian children could not understand why they were moved inland to detention camps, nor could West Coast children understand why their Japanese-Canadian classmates suddenly disappeared.

Youngsters found many interests to pursue. John Fedoruk and Rolland Lewis were two of many who built their own crystal sets and radios. They became amateur radio operators and both are still active amateurs. By the early 1930s, commercial radio was well established, and Dawn McKim recalled that her entire family listened to, among other programs, *Hockey Night in Canada* on Saturdays, as called by Foster Hewitt. Preschool children of the 1940s could listen five mornings a week to *Kindergarten of the Air* and weekly to *Maggie Muggins* and *Just Mary*, broadcast by the Canadian Broadcasting Corporation (CBC). Others enjoyed "It's a bird! It's a plane! It's Superman!" and "Hi! Ho! Silver, Away!" as well as *Tarzan of the Apes* or the buzzing sound of *The Green Hornet*. Saturday matinees at local theatres, be they westerns, swashbucklers, or adventures, provided fodder for games of the following week. Youngsters were so entranced by Tom Mix, Roy Rogers, Dale Evans, and other cowboy heroes that they dressed, walked, shot, and behaved like they believed their cowboy heroes would act.[81]

There was always reading. Books were regular Christmas and birthday gifts, and awards for good grades, regular Sunday school attendance, and memorizing catechism. Many children were avid readers, but access to books was often limited. Evelyn Slater MacLeod recalled there were only twelve books in her Alberta Willow Brook Rural School library, including *Black Beauty* and *The Last of the Mohicans,* and she read all twelve many times. Because the people of Winterton, Newfoundland, knew Nick Green liked to read, they regularly passed books and papers on to him; consequently he was exposed to a wide range of reading materials. There were few books in the McKim house, but there was a set of *The Book of Knowledge,* which the children read from interest and for school assignments.[82]

Stories such as R.L. Stevenson's *Treasure Island* or Jack London's *Call of the Wild* were adventures to dream about, and they provided ideas and plots for weeks of imaginative play. Fairy and folk tales and comic book characters such as Superman and Flash Gordon stimulated children's creative instincts. The *Boys' Own Annual, Chatterbox,* the *Girls' Own Annual,* and other books of this type were treasured. In addition, most religious denominations or organizations provided weekly or monthly papers or reading materials for each age group, and youngsters read the children's pages and serialized stories in the newspapers that came into their homes. Over the years the *Family Herald and Weekly Star* included in serialized form such authors as James Oliver Curwood, Arthur Conan Doyle, Lucy Maud Montgomery, and Ralph Connor. Such reading materials taught that right living and hard work ensured a happy and successful future.[83] And when one tired of reading, there were board games and card games to play with friends, siblings, and parents.[84]

Fun or More Fun?

Did children of pre-televison times really make their own fun? And did they have more fun than children today? The sources used for this study, and conversations with many "ancient ones," indicated nine characteristics that distinguish the idyllic world of childhood play and games in the days before television and electronic games became part of the culture of childhood.

Parents and teachers sent children out to play to get them out from under foot and to ensure youngsters got plenty of fresh air and exercise.

Children were free to play, to roam, and to explore both their rural and urban environments, and they felt free to do so.

Many of their games were physically active and often self-organized.

Toys and equipment were frequently limited, but children created or adapted whatever was needed to play the game.

Playing was often more important than winning; therefore, most available children were included in the games or activities. They could, however, also be keen competitors.

Domestic animals played important roles as companions and playmates, and wild birds and animals were sources of interest, food, and income.

Special days and holidays were welcome breaks from daily chores and seasonal tasks.

Although letter writers enjoyed being involved in organizations for children and youth, adults tended not to recall such organizations as a vital part of their childhood.

Children of pre-television times do not recall boredom as a companion or even a problem, as there was always something to do. Children for whom life was difficult or who were confined in detention camps, residential schools, or crowded inner-city areas, tried to adapt what time and materials they had to suit their situation.

In spite of their pleasant memories of childhoods between 1900 and the mid-1950s, those were challenging years for children as well as for their parents. Many were the children of immigrant families struggling to survive, and two world wars and a major economic depression certainly touched and, in many cases, affected them. Perhaps, as Leyshon observed, play helps children build optimism and hope. British journalist and dramatist, James M. Barrie explained it best when he observed, "God gave us a memory so that we could have roses in December."

But did they have more fun that children today? Historian Ludmilla Jordanova warns researchers to avoid the tendency to romanticize traditional values and to judge customs and actions of the past in terms of current values.[85] As Leyshon observed, "The natural progression of play activities has tended to grow more and more sophisticated over time."[86] After a visit to a large toy store one grandmother commented, "Everything is so fast, so noisy, and so expensive."[87] Children are bombarded with advertisements to purchase multiple numbers of collectible toys or cards that feature Disney characters, Beanie Babies, or sports figures, but they also have access to an ever-growing body of reading material. Both school and public libraries stock a diverse range of books, and teachers and librarians claim many children are avid readers and use books and the Internet in conjunction with classwork or in pursuing a special interest. Today's children are probably more knowledgeable and better informed on many topics than were their grandparents.

Some things, however, are unchanged. Children still play hopscotch, make snow angels, participate in various forms of tag, skip stones on water, make clothes for their dolls, and push them about in doll carriages. They also colour within lines and produce appropriate noises while pushing toy trucks or swooping airplanes. Children slide down snow-covered hills, throw snowballs at one another and at unwary passersby, play street hockey or soccer, and muck about with water, dirt, and stones. They search tidal pools for marine organisms and sloughs and ditches for pollywogs and frogs, and, where possible, build treehouses. They watch the skies for migrating birds. They fly kites and float bits of wood in puddles and gutters. Many traditional games and activities that are still played have been adapted to our changing society. In a few cases parents, teachers, and community recreation workers are teaching children traditional games from their own childhoods, including skipping rhymes and bouncing-ball games.

Today's children may be more sophisticated and knowledgeable than previous generations, but given the opportunity they play with the same creativity and zest as their grandparents. Children still burst through the door shouting, "Hey! Guess what we did today? We had so much fun!" The sparkle in their eyes, the joy on their faces, and the dishevelled state of their clothing, confirms they have had a wonderful time. When they are the "ancient ones," they will probably recall their own childhoods with nostalgia and be just as certain that they made their own fun.

NOTES

1 Friedrich Froebel, *The Education of Man* (New York: D. Appleton, 1909), 5.

2 Robert Bingham Downs, *Friedrich Froebel* (New York: G.K. Hall, 1978), 59-61.

3 Glynn A. Leyshon, "The Art of Play: Street Games in the Depression," *The Beaver* 79 (Aug.-Sept. 1999): 32-36; Neil Sutherland, *Growing Up: Childhood in English Canada from the Great War to the Age of Television* (Toronto: University of Toronto Press, 1997), 220-53.

4 Camilla Gryski, *Let's Play: Traditional Games of Childhood* (Toronto: Kids Can Press, 1995), 6-7; Iona and Peter Opie, *The Lore and Language of Schoolchildren* (Oxford: Clarendon Press, 1959); Soeur Marie Ursula, *Civilisation traditionelle des Lavalois* (Quebec: Les Presses Universitaires Laval, 1951), 95-111; D.N. Panabaker, "Pastimes among Pennsylvania Dutch in Waterloo," *Waterloo Historical Society* 19 (1931): 245-49.

5 Elliott West, *Growing Up with the Country: Childhood on the Western Frontier* (Albuquerque: University of New Mexico Press, 1989), xx-xxi.

6 Mary Tivy, "Nineteenth-Century Canadian Children's Games," *Material History Bulletin* (Spring 1985): 57-64; Janet Holmes, "Economic Choices and Popular Toys in the Nineteenth Century," Ibid: 51-56; Eaton's Mail Order Catalogues, Fall-Winter and Christmas editions, 1900 to 1955 indicated a wide range in both the quality and prices of toys available; Toys'R'Us indicates there are now only two Meccano sets available, one of which is a helicopter; Sarah Fraser, *Pasture Spruce: A Story of Rural Life in Nova Scotia at the Turn of the Century* (Halifax: Petheric Press, 1971), 37-38. Fraser recalled that the Eaton's Catalogue provided hours of entertainment, and was also a source of information for children.

7 Norah L. Lewis, *I Want to Join Your Club: Letters from Rural Children 1900-1920* (Waterloo: Wilfrid Laurier University Press, 1996).

8 West, xxi-xxii.

9 Gwyn Dow and June Factor, *Australian Childhood: An Anthology* (South Yarra: McPhee and Gribble), 1991.

10 George A. Dickinson, *The Country Boy* (Toronto: Briggs, 1907), 9. Ontario Archives, Toronto, Pamphlet, No. 4. "All this [agricultural] work is so much fun the youngster will not recognize when work ends and play begins. The country boy has his work, play and study so combined and sandwiched that the overworking of one activity never occurs." It seems unlikely Dickinson was reared on a farm; David C. Jones, "'There Is Some Power about the Land' — The Western Agrarian Press and Country Life Ideology," *Journal of Canadian Studies* 17 (Fall 1982): 96-107.

11 Sutherland, *Growing Up*, 115-18, 142-67; Neil Sutherland, "'I Can't Recall When I Didn't Help': The Working Lives of Pioneering Children in Twentieth-Century British Columbia," *Histoire sociale/Social History* 24 (Nov. 1991): 263-88.

12 Lewis, *I Want to Join Your Club*, 131, 170, 175, 171, 178, 182; Ben W. Powell, *Labrador by Choice* (St. John's: Jesperson Press, 1979), 1-8; Sing Lim, *A West Coast Chinese Boy* (Montreal: Tundra, 1979), 30-31, 35; Interview with Donna Ebbutt, May 2000.

13 *Family Herald and Weekly Star,* January 13, 1904. It is interesting that this letter was published, as it was unusual for an agrarian newspaper to print anything that reflected rural life in a negative way.

14 Sing Lim, 35; Wayson Choy, *Paper Shadows: A Chinatown Childhood* (Toronto: Viking, 1999), 98, 282. Choy knew of children who were abused; Barry Broadfoot, *The Pioneer Years: Memories of the Settlers Who Opened the West* (Markham: Paperjacks, 1978), 182-83; Some children had time to play, but no one with whom to play. See Charles Ritchie, *My Grandfather's House: Scenes of Childhood and Youth* (Toronto: Macmillan, 1987).

15 Jacqueline Bliss, "Seamless Lives: Pioneer Women of Saskatoon 1883-1903," *Saskatchewan History* 43 (Aug. 1992): 90-91.

16 Eliane Leslau Silverman, *The Last Best West: Women on the Alberta Frontier, 1880-1930* (Montreal: Eden Press, 1984), 16.

17 Charles H. McKenzie, "Growing Up in Alberta. Part One," *Alberta History* 37 (Summer 1989): 15-18.

18 Isabelle (Doyle) Daley, "My Childhood Days on the Farm," *The Island Magazine* 30 (Fall/Winter 1991): 3-8.

19 Interview with Don Clay, February 1999; W.O. Mitchell, *Who Has Seen the Wind* (Toronto: Macmillan, 1947). Mitchell captures the essence and spirit of the freedom of childhood, but he also touches on some darker experiences.

20 James Gray, *The Boy from Winnipeg* (Toronto: Macmillan, 1970), 12-14, 46; Silverman, 23. Doris Spring and her friends bobsledded for blocks down local streets.

21 Discussion with Ina Trudgeon, 1999.

22 Leyshon, 32-36.

23 Lorraine Blashill, *Remembering the '50s* (Victoria: Orca Press, 1997), v-vii.

24 Joy Kogawa, *Obasan* (Toronto: Penguin Books, 1983), 127-31, 138-42; Shizuye Takashima, *A Child in Prison Camp* (Montreal: Tundra Books, 1971), n.p.

25 Basil H. Johnston, *Indian School Days* (Toronto: Key Porter Books, 1988). Johnston describes his life in the Spanish, Ontario, Residential School for Boys; residents often referred to residential school as "jail."

26 Shirley Sterling, *My Name Is Seepeetza* (Vancouver: Groundwood Books, 1982). Although most residential schools operated in the same regimented manner, there were variations in activities and programs among schools.

27 Discussion with Freda Mallory, March 1998; artist William Kurelek illustrated both the freedom to play and the constraints of work in *A Prairie Boy's Winter and Summer* (Montreal: Tundra, 1973); Brubacher, 41-42.

28 Gryski, 5-6.

29 Edith Fowke, *Red Rover, Red Rover: Children's Games Played in Canada* (Toronto: Doubleday, 1988).

30 Gray, 16; Leyshon, 31-36; Discussion with Freda Mallory, 1998; Broadfoot, 195-96.

31 Discussion with Ina Trudgeon, 1999.

32 Discussion with Bernadette Yuan, 2001.

33 Leyshon, 34.

34 Evelyn Slater McLeod, "School Days at Willow Brook," *The Beaver* 32 (1981): 40-45; Discussion with Arline Huminuk, 2001.

35 Discussions with Neil Sutherland and Fred Greaves, 2000.

36 Gray, 12-14; Carl J. Buchanan, "A Wintery Day on the Homestead," *The Beaver* 307 (1976): 6-9. Weather permitting, the Buchanan boys skied, or tobogganed down a long steep hill, or played hockey on the hard-packed barnyard. Indoors, Carl and his brothers played blackjack, King Pedro or cribbage; Ted Logie, *Ted Logie Tells Okanagan Tales* (Penticton: Logie, 1967), 20-21, 143.

37 Jean Cochrane, *One-Room School in Canada* (Toronto: Fitzhenry and Whiteside, 1981), 11; Not only were skates traded around, but also

other sports equipment. Trading hockey equipment is still a regular practice.

38 Discussion with Harry Sullivan, 2000. The students, grades 1 to 8, of Saskatchewan's Sweetwater Rural School #1156, with some help from their fathers, packed the snow, put up boards for the rink walls, and hauled water about two miles to flood the rink. Inner tubes were a wonderful source of rubber bands, and were used to repair myriad items in the pre-duct-tape era; Henry Barone's memories are of open-air rinks in Toronto parks.

39 Ken Dryden, "Soul on Ice: A Century of Canadian Hockey," *The Beaver* 80 (Dec. 2000-Jan. 2001): 1-23; young players bought, and still buy, the sweaters that not only reflect their team preference, but also bear the number of their favourite player. See Roch Carrier, *The Hockey Sweater* (Montreal: Tundra, 1984).

40 Johnston, 76-77.

41 Discussion with Glen Tibbitts, 2001.

42 Johnston, 63; Bryan Eddington, "Little Brother of War," *The Beaver* 80 (Oct.-Nov. 2000): 9-14; Celia Haig-Brown, *Resistance and Renewal: Surviving the Indian Residential School* (Vancouver: Tillicum, 1989), 70-72.

43 Sterling, 36. Although the dance troupe was very good and received many awards and compliments on their dancing ability, Sterling felt some dancers do not recall the dance troupe as a positive experience.

44 Helen Porter, *Below the Bridge* (St. John's: Breakwater Books, 1979), 77-78.

45 Bernice McDonough, "Pioneer Playtime," *Pioneer News* (March 1991): 2.

46 John C. Charyk, *The Little White Schoolhouse* (Saskatoon: Western Producer Books, 1968), 170.

47 Fredelle Bruser Maynard, *Raisins and Almonds* (Don Mills: Paper Jacks, 1973), 73-75.

48 Fred Greaves recalls yoyo and bolo bat demonstrations and competitions held in Vancouver parks and on street corners near schools.

49 McDonough, 1.

50 Sterling, 37-39; Ruby Stonehouse, Maple Leaf Club, *Family Herald and Weekly Star*, January 2, 1918.

51 "Aunt Cicely's Sewing Class, Rag Doll, and Clothes," *Family Herald and Weekly Star*, November 14, 1900.

52 Evelyn Robson Strahlendorf, *The Charlton Standard Catalogue of Canadian Dolls*. 2nd ed. (Toronto: Charlton Press, 1992); One of the best-known Canadian dolls was "Eaton's Beauty," first manufactured in

1900. Others dolls included Shirley Temple (1934), Dionne quintuplets, and Barbara Ann Scott. There were also Canadian paper dolls printed in the *Canadian Home Journal,* July 1928-April 1939. One example is "Harold and His Playmates," by Grace G. Drayton. His outfits included rompers, hat, shoes, wagon, dog and rabbit; McDonough, 1-2.

53 The dolls and teddy bears given young residential school children were usually supplied by women's or girls' church groups.

54 Both Fred Greaves and Bud Phillips recall the thrill of the soapbox derby. As of 1991, soapbox races were reinstatement in Vancouver. The 11th Annual Soapbox Derby was held June 24, 2001.

55 Olive O'Brien, *Running with the Wind* (Fernwood: Harrison, 1977), 51; children not only played house, school, and store, but they also incorporated into their play family, community, and national events such as weddings, coronations, journeys, rodeos, journeys, sports events, plots of movies they had seen, and the books they had read.

56 Nancy J. Turner, *Plant Technology of First Peoples of British Columbia* (Vancouver: University of British Columbia Press, 1998), 14, 34-35; With a lot of ingenuity and hard work, Jack and Ivy Moulton made a cart that their pony could pull, but the cart would not turn; Parents often made toys for their children.

57 Conversation with Neil Bramble, 2001.

58 Conversations with Eileen Campbell, Glen Sullivan, and Dick Saunders; Conversation with Smitty Glover, 2001. Materials for the kite were easily accessible, and the instructions were simple; Slater McLeod, 40-46.

59 Leyshon, 34; Jack Driedger, "A Homemade Merry-Go-Round," *Folklore: Saskatchewan's Yesterdays Personified* 20, 2 (Winter 1998-99): 24; and "How We Made a Slingshot," *Folklore* (Spring 1998): 27.

60 Discussion with Laurena Saunders, 2000; discussion with Ina Trudgeon; Gary L. Saunders, *Rattles and Steadies: Memoirs of a Gander River Man* (St. John's: Breakwater Press, 1986), 22-23.

61 Barbara E. Kelcey, "The Great Gopher War," *The Beaver* 79 (June-July 1999): 16-21; James M. Minifie, *Homesteader: A Prairie Boyhood Recalled* (Toronto: Macmillan, 1972), 103-105, 152-53; C. Howard Shillington, *Return to Avondale* (West Vancouver: Evvard), 72-75. The amount paid per gopher tail appeared to vary by municipality. Adults recall rates that ranged from two cents to ten cents.

62 Howard White, *Spilsbury's Coast* (Madeira Park: Harbour Publishing, 1988), 23-24. Spilsbury acquired an old .55 caliber Swiss Army rifle from a neighbour. Guns were also available from *Eaton's Cata-*

logue, general and hardware stores, and gun shops, and they were passed down in the family and sold or traded among neighbours. Farmers, ranchers, and sheep herders regularly carried rifles to discourage predators. As poultry flocks were often the responsibility of women, they learned to shoot to protect their flocks. In case the small hunter ran out of pellets for his or her air rifle, a loud noise could be produced by putting a wooden match down the barrel and pulling the trigger.

63 D.H. Grigg, *From One to Seventy* (Vancouver: Mitchell, 1953), 1-3. Grigg, a child from a poor family, reported, that in about 1900, he and other youngsters used guns to hunt rabbits to feed the family; Dave Aldous, "Rabbit Drives," *Folklore* 20, 2 (Winter 1998-99): 21. As a boy, Aldous hunted rabbits for profit by shooting them with his .22 or snaring them. Jackrabbits were deemed pests because they ate crops, gardens, and young saplings. Aldous described a rabbit drive in which rabbits were driven into a V-shaped pen and then killed.

64 The four Wray girls hunted and fished to feed the family while their brothers worked as loggers and fishers.

65 Johnston, 13-15.

66 Fran Newman and Claudette Boulanger, *Hooray for Today* (Richmond Hill: North Winds Press, 1979). The authors look at twenty-four festivals and special days that are celebrated in Canada; Joan Adams and Becky Thomas, *Floating Schools and Frozen Inkwells: The One-Room Schools of British Columbia* (Madeira Park: Harbour Publishing, 1985), 85-95. The authors described the activities and excitement of special days in a school and a community; Sterling, 30-31; Cochrane, 111-12, 156.

67 Dale Simmons, "Community Pride on the Line: Rivalries at Sports Days," *Folklore* 19 (Summer 1998): 18-19; William J. Browne, *Eighty-four Years a Newfoundlander* (St. John's: Dicks Press, 1981), 15-16.

68 Margaret Parker, "Behind the Sateen Curtain," in Hugh A. Dempsey, ed., *Christmas in the West* (Saskatoon: Western Producer Books, 1982), 141; Amy J. Ross, "A Hard Times Christmas," in Dempsey, *Christmas*, 113-16. Ross offered readers practical suggestions for gifts that could be made from materials at hand.

69 John C. Charyk, *The Biggest Day of the Year: The Old-Time Christmas Concert* (Saskatoon: Prairie Books, 1985), 5.

70 Maynard, 27-37.

71 John C. Charyk, *Syrup Pails and Gopher Tails: Memories of the One-Room School* (Saskatoon: Western Producer Press, 1983), 118-19. Charyk includes copies of the instructions for ordering gifts, and a sample of

"Eaton's Order Form for Christmas Gifts"; Agnes Schendelka, "Concert at Flanders," *Folklore* 20, 2 (Winter 1998-99): 14; Silverman, 21; Adams and Thomas, 86-90.

72 Johnston, 77-78.

73 Takashima, n. p.

74 Sing Lim, 54-55.

75 M. Lucille Marr, "Church Teen Clubs, Feminized Organizations? Tuxis Boys, Trail Rangers, and Canadian Girls in Training," *Historical Studies in Education/Revue d'histoire de l'education* 3 (1991): 249-67; Margaret Prang, "'The Girl God Would Have Me Be': The Canadian Girls in Training, 1915-1939," *Canadian Historical Review* 66 (1985): 154-84; A number of organizations were imported from Great Britain and the United States, but the CGIT, Tuxis Boys, and Trail Rangers were home-grown; Veronica Strong-Boag, *The New Day Recalled: Lives of Girls and Women in English Canada 1919-1939* (Toronto: Copp Clark Pitman, 1988), 28; David Howell and Peter Lindsay, "Social Gospel and the Young Boy Problem," *Canadian Journal of the History of Sports* 17 (May 1986): 75-87. Although several organizations, including CGIT, were sponsored by specific religious institutions, membership followed friendship as much as denominational lines. Many of these organizations provided books of games and activities for leaders. *Group Games* (Toronto: Religious Education Council of Canada, undated).

76 Nan Bourgeon, *Rubber Boots Are for Dancing* (Cloverdale: D.W. Friesen, 1979), 109. The Extension Department of the University of British Columbia held travelling schools for farm boys and girls who were not able to go to high school. Lessons were given during the day, and in the evening there was physical education, folk dancing, puppet shows, and community singing. Girls were taught rug-making, cooking, and sewing; boys were taught to handle farm machinery, welding, blacksmithing, working with farm animals, and agriculture; some of the present members of the Beatty, Saskatchewan, Calf Club, formed in 1939, are the third generation of their family to be involved.

77 Don Morrow, "The Strathcona Trust in Ontario 1911-1939," *The Canadian Journal of Sport and Education* 8 (May 1977): 72-90; Desmond Morton, "The Cadet Movement in the Moment of Canadian Militarism," *Journal of Canadian Studies* 13 (Summer 1979): 56-68; Father Bob Ogle, *North/South Calling* (Saskatoon: Fifth House, 1987), 12. "I loved everything about Cadets—the airplanes, the courses we took, the wireless, everything."

78 Jean Browne, "Junior Red Cross," *Papers and Proceedings of the Conference on Child Welfare*, 1923; Alan R. Young, "'We throw the torch': Canadian Memorials of the Great War and the Mythology of Heroic Sacrifice," *Journal of Canadian Studies* 14 (Winter 1989-90): 5-29; Norah Lewis, "'Isn't This a Terrible War?' The Attitude of Children to Two World Wars," *Historical Studies in Education/Revue d'Histoire de l' Education* 7 (1995): 193-215.

79 Nancy M. Sheehan, "The IODE, the School and World War I." Paper presented at the Canadian History of Education Conference, October 1983, Vancouver B.C.; Manfred Prokop, "Canadianization of Immigrant Children: Role of the Rural Elementary School in Alberta, 1900-1930," *Alberta History* 32 (1989): 1-10; Neil Sutherland, "The Triumph of Formalism: Elementary Schooling in Vancouver from the 1920s to the 1960s," *B.C. Studies* 69-70 (Spring/Summer 1989): 181. Patriotic displays and decorations were a common feature in classrooms; "'League of the Empire' — An Imperial Union of Schools through Schools' and Pupils' Correspondence, 1922." Ontario Archives, RG2 P3; "Magna Carta Day: A Sign Post Raised by English Speaking Nations on the Path of Civilization to World Peace," 1937; Violet McNaughton Papers, Saskatchewan Archives Board, Regina; Saunders, 37. Saunders commented on the British focus of his textbooks; Blashill, 48. Saluting the flag, singing "O Canada" and "God Save the Queen," and reciting "The Lord's Prayer" were daily routines in many Canadian schools; J. Stuart Prentice, "History in a Prairie School," *The Beaver* 302 (Autumn 1972): 20-25.

80 Kogawa, 152.

81 Diane Schoemperlen, *Hockey Night in Canada* (Kingston: Quarry, 1987); Wayson Choy, 69-71, 87-88. Choy, and many other children walked, talked, dressed, and behaved as they believed cowboys and cowgirls behaved.

82 Slater McLeod, 40-46; Interview with Nick Green, July 1999; Walter Wicks, *Memories of the Skeena* (Seattle: Saanichton, 1976), 22-25.

83 Children's favourite authors included R.M. Ballantyne, Capt. Frederick Marryat, G.A. Henty, and Ralph Connor (Rev. Charles Gordon); *Eaton's Mail Order Catalogue, Fall and Winter, 1908-1909* listed seventy-five adventure books; four Horatio Alger books; thirty-six Henty books, eighteen Ballantyne books, twenty-eight Elsie Dinsmore books, and eleven Peter Rabbit books. *Eaton's Mail Order Catalogue, Fall and Winter 1915-16*, included eleven Talbot Baines Reed "tales of snap and ginger, clean and wholesome, the kind a manly boy thoroughly enjoys"; twelve of the Boy Scout Series by Lieu-

tenant Howard Payson (John Henry Goldfarp); nine of The Boy Allies Series by Clair Wallace Hayes (Robert L. Drake); *Eaton's Catalogue 1900-01* also listed the popular *Girls' Own Annual, Boys' Own Annual, Chums,* and *Chatterbox*; Shane Peacock, "Leslie McFarlane: The Canadian Writer Who Was Franklin W. Dixon," *The Beaver* 77 (June-July 1997): 24-31.

84 Rosemary Neering, *Settlement of the West* (Toronto: Fitzhenry and Whiteside, 1974), 52-53. Neering lists five hundred, flinch, checkers, chess, nations, tiddlywinks, and dominoes as games played by both children and adults; Jean F. Fahlman, "Games We Used to Play," *Folklore* 19, 2 (Spring 1998): 23.

85 Ludmilla Jordanova, "Children in History: Concepts of Nature and Society," in Geoffrey Scarre, ed. *Children, Parents and Politics* (Cambridge: Cambridge University Press. 1989), 3-24.

86 Leyshon, 35.

87 "Too many toys can hurt kids, study says," *Vancouver Sun,* March 16, 2001. The article mentions recent studies in the United States and England that indicate giving young children too many toys, or toys of the wrong type, can be harmful as it may impede their ability to focus on a task.

Go Outside and Play

THE FAIR LAND

Reprinted with the permission of Alan Bell from Betty Bell.
(Victoria: Sono Nis, 1982).

In 1906, the Bell Family moved to South Saanich, Vancouver Island. For Betty and her sister, Helen, it was an idyllic world.

Memories of Saanich crowd upon me and, to this day, upon hearing the staccato chatter of a flicker, I am drawn back all those years to one secluded glade in our wood which gained special favour in our eyes. This mossy nook between long-fallen trees, which held so much charm for two small girls, also especially attracted the flickers because of the presence of rotting tree trunks in the grove, assuring them of a constant supply of grubs. So, for very different reasons, we children and those hungry birds alighting with a blaze of orange-red shared a deep-seated appreciation of the glade.

Trilliums chose damp and shady corners — their usual preference — but Shooting Stars, which to us were "Peacocks" selected dryer and less sheltered glades within the bushland to display their orchid coloured blooms. Many other flowers flourished, each in its own season — honeysuckle, syringa, Indian paint brush, all the vetches and clovers, and an infinite number of minute blossoms clinging to the earth. Rarer delights were the orange tiger lilies, wild columbines, and pungent chocolate lilies (locally known as "snake lilies"), their dark brown petal spattered with greenish yellow, looking as though someone had just

35

shaken an unwashed paintbrush at them. Why, I wonder, did we and other children in the neighbourhood so persistently apply names other than the orthodox ones to the birds and flowers of our youth?

We had endless time to absorb all that encompassed us, and countless hours of freedom and pleasure were barely interrupted by a minimum of simple chores, such as setting forth daily for some neighbouring farm to fetch milk in the empty tin which one of us clutched. This was a brassy-looking receptacle with a metal handle, originally emanating from the grocery store when filled with several pounds of lard, and still bearing its commercial label. These excursions permitted investigation of whatever proved interesting along the way as no time was strictly set for our return, and inevitably the distractions were boundless.

The marvels, discoveries and joys of those early days were endless, and memories of them come back sometimes faintly as if being dragged from oblivion, or sometimes in an almost overwhelming wave, but whether barely recollecting or suddenly engulfed by the past, the feeling is almost without exception happy and cherishable. Above everything else, an immense sense of quiet and leisure haunts all my earliest memories of Saanich.

[The Wilkinson boys added a new dimension to games played.]

The boys had been given a magnificent collection of lead soldiers, consisting of infantry, cavalry, artillery, highlanders, troops with swarthy faces wearing turbans, (some of whom were mounted on camels), and a great deal of military equipment, due to which we came to enjoy warlike games with soldiers just as much as the boys across the road, and took great pleasure in being introduced to a totally new and different occupation.

Mrs. Bovill's niece, Miss Wishart — an American — introduced Helen and me to what became a favorite occupation of ours for a few years. She subscribed to the *Ladies' Home Journal* and at that time the magazine was inserting a coloured page in each issue illustrating a paper doll named Lottie and her varied outfits. Each month Lottie's extensive wardrobe was added to, conforming to the changes of season and running the gamut from a decidedly discreet Edwardian bathing suit to winter furs. This page, presented to us regularly by Miss Wishart, afforded countless hours of pleasure while we cut out and tried on the doll's new clothes.

Later on, inspired by Lottie, we began to create our own paper dolls, drawing and hand colouring them and then designing their apparel — probably weird and clumsy creations. Painting of any kind was one of our regular and always available pleasures during the greater part of childhood; most often brush drawings in watercolour of favorite flowers and autumn leaves were the outcome, but there were also occasional excursions into landscapes, some displaying magnificent but improbable sunsets.

HAPPY MOUNTAINEERS

Maple Leaf Club, *Family Herald and Weekly Star*
November 16, 1904

Anna V.M. Robinson
THE MATINEE GIRL (14)
Rossland, B.C.

Dear Old M.L.C.:

It is about time I wrote to you again. We have had lovely weather here until yesterday, when it turned very cold, and last night while the people of Rossland were sleeping, old King Snow and his helper, Jack Frost, were doing their work on a couple of mountains close by here. Mount Roberts especially, from the peak down about half way, is covered with snow, and oh! it looks so cold.

On Labour Day, September 1, a couple of my friends and myself went down to the Sheep Creek Falls on the engine. We had a good time with camera and kodak and took some fine views and pictures. How many of the members have ever ridden on an engine? I think it was great fun. Then a week after, we (the same three) went to the top of Red Mountain, a small hill here, being only 5,000 feet. Last November 4th I climbed to the peak of

Mount Roberts. The mountain is 6,500 feet above sea level, and I can tell you I was a little bit tired when I got home. There were patches of snow here and there, and in it I saw quite a few bear tracks, but did not see the grizzly. The altitude at the top is so high I could hardly breathe. Dad put a flag-pole up there on June 4, 1900, and nearly every holiday he goes up and hoists the flag. We can just barely see it down town when it is flying. The first flag he put up he left flying for a week, and when he went up to bring it down, it was torn to ribbons and the ends were braided tighter than any person could every braid — the wind's work.

I have two pets, a dog Rover, 11 years old and a kitten named Bedelia, after that popular Irish coon song.

Will Vade Mecum please write to me when she has time, and also Kathleen from Ireland?

With best wishes to the M.L.C.

GOOD TIMES AT OAKVILLE

Maple Leaf Club, *Family Herald and Weekly Star*
September 14, 1904

Fanny Heeks
Oakville, Ont.

We play many games at school, but there is a branch of the Grand Trunk Railway near the school, and woods almost all the way around, it is more interesting to be outside the school yard than in. In the winter we slide down banks, in the summer we gather wild flowers, paddle in the creek or have picnics. One year we had a raft, which the boys made from drift-wood. Oh! what times we had on the raft. Many were the accidents and upsets which those near-by trees witnessed, if they could but tell you of them. One boy climbed out on a branch of a willow which hung over the pond. He had his feet over the branch, while he hung on with both hands. The limb was limber and tough, and behold! e'er George knew it, he was sitting on the surface. Another boy fell off the raft, and all that was visible was his head and right shoulder.

One day—a bitter cold, winter day—seven girls besides myself went over to the woods. We got as far as the creek, when two girls stepped on the ice, but passed on no further. I jumped next while the rest followed. As the last stepped down the ice gave way. All tried to stay on the largest piece, but it broke, sending us in all directions. I got on the opposite side and pulled another girl after me. All except one girl got back again; but she was utterly helpless. Imagine her sitting on a piece of ice in the middle of the creek, and wringing her hands. However, she got out with the aid of two boys who came along.

THE ABSOLUTE FREEDOM WE HAD

The Clay boys spent most of their growing years on the southern end of Vancouver Island. Don, the eldest of the boys (born a year apart), looks back over seven decades.

My earliest memories are of our three and a half acre place at Sooke. Our playmates were the younger members of the large Pontius family whose property was accessible through our back fence. The Pontius' big barn with its loft and empty stalls, was one of our favorite places to play. Sooke Harbour was only a half hour's walk away, and my mother used to take us down there to paddle when we were little.

Two summers in particular stand out above all others. Because my dad worked for Sooke Harbour Fishing and Packing, he could arrange to take us camping on site when he worked the East Sooke traps. In front of our tent was a steep slope covered with dry grass, and Dad built little sleds for us to slide down. This really provided some hairy scary runs. How we didn't break our necks is anybody's guess! The beaches were a source of an endless variety of treasures including flotsam and agates.

The following summer we went out to the Muir Creek traps, out towards Jordan River. That summer my Mother found an abandoned seal pup on the beach and made quite a pet of it. My dad fashioned a collar for it and strung a wire across the mouth of Muir Creek with a sliding chain on it so the seal could swim and feed himself. He would come out and sit on my mother's lap. I even have a picture of it. But there was a small outfit cutting cordwood up in Muir Creek. They loaded the wood on to a scow, and one night a tug came in at high tide and towed out the scow. Unfortunately, our seal went with it.

In 1927, we moved to Ocean Falls where my Dad got a good job as a bricklayer with Crown Zellerbach Pulp and Paper Company. Here fishing was one of the main attractions for us. There was a great big company store right down on the wharf, and a combination storm drain and sewer outfall came out just off the waterside corner. And that water was just teeming with fish. We used to call them 'sewer cod'. We would rig tackle (hand lines) and we'd pull in a fish every time we dropped a line in the water. We spent hours down there. The store provided our main source of income for tackle and candy—we would break up packing cases for kindling and then pedal the wood about town.

Later, my Dad built a dory, which we subsequently moved up to Link Lake behind the dam. On weekends he would row us out where creeks ran in off the hillside, usually providing a gravel bar you could land on. These were great places to picnic and fish. The water was so clear you could easily see the trout feeding where the stream ran into the lake. My youngest brother Leonard was fantastically lucky in fishing; he could out-fish Eric and me two or three to one. I have never seen anyone his match. My mother also had this ability.

Another summer jaunt was to take the trail to Martin Valley to the old farm were the Company had (unsuccessfully) tried running a dairy herd. A beautiful creek ran through the farm where you could see large steelhead resting in the pools. In summer, this trail was the greatest berry picking patch you ever saw with luscious huckleberries, blueberries, and salmonberries.

In the latter part of '29 we moved back to Victoria and lived right across the street from the George Jay School. It was rough undeveloped land, semi-open with lots of broom, shrubbery and rose bushes. This was our haunt for playing cowboys and Indians. We all had hand-carved guns, and we raised hell over there in a great way. On the other side of where we lived was the Royal Athletic Park where professional baseball games were held regularly. We could not afford our entrance fees, but there were lots of knot holes in the fence providing economical viewing.

About a year later my folks moved to Craigflower Road in Victoria West. We were not far from the Gorge water, a great area to prowl around in. A street car track ran along Craigflower Avenue in front of our place, and we children couldn't resist putting pennies and bottle caps on the track to flatten them out.

Boy with Newfoundland dog and cart, undated (Provincial Archives of Newfoundland and Labrador [A32-58]).

We kids used to hike all the way to downtown Victoria to a theatre called the "Columbia" on Government Street. Children could see the matinee for a dime. We tried not to miss the Saturday matinees because they were always preceded by a running serial. It was regularly updated, but each episode ended in such a hair raising situation we just had to see what happened next!

Another treat was to go around behind the Columbia to Broad Street where the North-Western Creamery made milk shakes beyond belief! they were so rich and flavourful, a full pint served in a metal container. The shake was so thick you could stand a spoon up in it. It was nigh impossible to suck it up through the thin straws of those days.

In less than two years my folks moved out to Metchosin. This was a wonderful place to grow up as we had access to Witty's, Taylor's and Weir's beaches. Our favorite was Witty's as the tide went out anywhere from a quarter to a half mile. Besides beach combing we used to wade out and spear flounders and crabs. Once we found an old log, around twelve feet long, that had enough stubs of roots to stabilize it. We poled and paddled it off the beach for hours at a time. We managed to retain that log a full month or so before the tide finally carried it away. In the summer when the tide came in across the flats, the water became so warm it was just wonderful. The best swimming spot was right in the narrows where the water flowed into Witty's lagoon.

Immediately across the narrows was the house of Colonel Yeats. I became quite chummy with his son Denis who had, of all things, a beautiful little twelve foot dugout canoe. It was a traditional design and shape, but it had been rigged for rowing by installing oarlocks. This proved to be a real seaworthy craft, even in lumpy conditions. Denis and I would gather up a can of pork and beans, maybe peaches or pears, two bottles of stone ginger beer, some pilot bread and butter, a frying pan, matches, and then we'd head for the canoe. We would row out to the Haystack Islands off the end of Albert Head Peninsula. We'd go ashore, build a fire, and have a mug-up before prowling all over the islands. In those days everybody used to throw their trash overboard off boats so the whole coast was littered with flotsam which made very interesting beachcombing.

My folks then decided to sell the family business and move to Happy Valley Road, between Metchosin and Luxton. This place opened a whole new vista to us kids. We started acquiring .22 rifles. The place was alive with rabbits that ate everything we planted. It took two years of spirited hunting, aided by our old dog Mickie, to clean the critters out. Instead of buying candy, our hard earned money went towards buying .22 ammunition. We were not satisfied with shooting stationary targets, but advanced to moving ones. We tossed tin cans into the creek and swung others from tree branches. We even advanced to hitting tin plates thrown edgewise into the air. No one would come to our place until it was dark, and even then they weren't too sure. My brother Len nearly nailed me one time. He came up on the back porch, while I was in the kitchen, yelling, "Stick 'em up or I'll plug you." And the damn gun went off, but luckily missed me.

I can't recall other youngsters being into guns like us. My mother was a crack shot having grown up with a .22 on the East Sooke farm.

In our very early teens bicycles featured as the big item in our lives. We scrounged and traded parts locally to build our own bikes. One of our favorite jaunts was to ride through Metchosin and on to the Rocky Point Road. At the second crossing of the C.N.R. tracks we turned right on Matheson Lake. At this point we would usually eat lunch, maybe fish, and occasionally ride as far as Roches Cove where the track crossed Gillespie Road. This now abandoned railway grade forms part of the well known Galloping Goose recreational trail.

We took a more extensive sixty-seven mile ride one Sunday over the following route: pedalling over to Langford, then north up the Island Highway to the Shawnigan Lake turnoff, then downhill to Shawnigan turning right here, with a further down hill ride to Mill Bay. Here we were at sea level and faced the long uphill climb to the Malahat summit at twelve hundred feet elevation. From this point, with the exception of Goldstream Hill, we had a lot of elevation to lose. We really flew down the Malahat Mountain, passing many cars enroute. At that time, although paved, the surface was very narrow, no shoulders and quite twisty. Our bikes were ill equipped to handle hills. They were only single speed, and had the inefficient coaster brake on the rear wheel only.

My most pleasant memory of my childhood is the absolute freedom we had, absolute freedom! We could do anything we wanted. We weren't destructive, but we could roam all over the country. It was ours to look at and enjoy. There was so much to see and do. We never had time hanging on our hands!

❧

A TRIP ON A STEAMER

Summer Days, *Family Herald and Weekly Star*
August 2, 1911

Helga Erlindson (13)
Reykjavik, Man.

On Victoria Day last year a party of girls of my own age embarked on a large steamer. The weather was calm and, as the boat glided near the river's bank, we could enjoy the beautiful scenery.

At first it passed many houses that were situated on open plains and could be seen well from afar. We saw many trees such as pine, spruce and maple growing on the bank.

At last the boat landed at an island. Here we disembarked and the captain promised to pick us up when he came back after going a little distance to get lumber. On this isle was a little cottage with ivy climbing up to the roof. In front was a little garden decorated with flowering plants. The cottage had once been occupied by an English family who had lately moved to England.

For a long time we wandered up and down this lovely little island, which we knew not the name of, but determined to call it "Gull Island" as the wild sea-gulls were so numerous there.

At last, being tired of wandering we sat down under the shade of a large pine tree to eat our lunch. A little rivulet flowed rapidly onward just before our feet. There were plenty of birch trees there so each of us made a cup out of the birch-bark and drank from its fresh waters. When our meal was over we went to explore the cottage.

Again we went to roam until it was eight o'clock in the evening, and we were getting uneasy about the steamer. We thought the captain had forgotten his promise and left us alone on the isle. Hours passed on and it was now quite late so we went into the house to rest. At first we were afraid we could never get away from the isle, but as we were tired after wandering about all day we soon fell asleep. At four o'clock next morning we were awakened by the captain who had been delayed at the lumber mills.

We got safely home, but we never forgot the good time we had wandering on lovely "Gull Island."

WILD FLOWERS

Maple Leaf Club, *Family Herald and Weekly Star*
June 28, 1911

WILD ROSE (15)
B.C.
(Thanks for the lovely flowers, Wild Rose. — Ed.)

Dear Maple Leaves:

As father is a subscriber to the Family Herald and Weekly Star, I thought I would write. I wrote once before, but my letter found the waste-basket. I think all Canadian children should be proud of the Maple Leaf Club. I will take for my subject "Flowers." I am a lover of them. I don't think there is anything so dainty as the rose. Look at the beautiful petals, and the exquisitely shaped leaves. There are also the dear little violets that grow in the swamps and near beautiful streams. What dainty hues they have! I am sending you some violets, wood clematis, and siwash potato blossoms. The latter are found in large quantities near marshy places, and they resemble a lady's slipper. The Indians of this country dig them the same as you would the cultivated ones, and they are eaten as food. The are mealy like Irish potatoes. They have a sweet flavor. This fall I'll send you some. If anyone would like to correspond with me, I should be very pleased.

WE WERE FREE TO ROAM

Between 1934 and 1949, the Scott family lived on a homestead near Pierceland, Saskatchewan. Eileen Scott Campbell recalls her girlhood.

As children we used to make our own entertainment. We climbed tall trees until the trees started to bend, then we'd tie ourselves on or just hang on, bounce up and down, sway back and forth, and sometimes swing from tree to tree. My brother got pretty good at it. In winter we jumped off the barn roof into deep snow drifts, hitched the dog to the sled, played fox and goose, and made angels in the snow. My dad made us skis. He steamed boards to shape the runners and then put straps over them to hold them on our feet. We also had homemade sleighs for tobogganing and sliding, and snowshoes, but I never mastered snowshoes.

For the summer, Dad cut the top off a good-sized tree, put a bolt through a big plank into the tree. Then we'd go round and round, one on each end of the plank. I suppose it was actually a merry-go-round. He put a board over a sawhorse and that was our teeter totter, and he hung ropes from tree branches to make swings.

My two brothers, my cousin and I were playmates. We would harness up our billy goat in dog harness, hitch him to a little cart we made, and then drive him around. We also had a dog, and the dog and goat would come a half mile down the road to meet us when we were walking home from school. It was odd to see them together—they were an odd couple.

I had lots of nice dolls that my aunt sent me from England. I wasn't much for dolls, but two friends came to visit occasionally and I played dolls with them and had tea parties. But I never could understand why they wanted to play dolls because they just undressed them and then dressed them again. I thought that was stupid! The dolls looked so pretty, so why tear them apart? I did enjoy the tea parties though. We'd crack some raw eggs into a dish, mix them all up with some wild berries and drink it just the way it was—raw eggs!!!

In the summertime we'd build playhouses from poles—a teepee like the Indians used to build. Then we'd weave cardboard in and out around the bottom to keep the wind out and make it comfortable inside. We used orange boxes and things like that, for our cupboards. Then we'd invite the boys for our tea parties—they were supposed to be our company. Our parents had a smoke house, and sometimes we'd go into the smoke house and snitch a little smoked pork for our tea party. I used to make mud pies and bake them in the sun.

In the spring we played hopscotch and skipped. We also made rafts that we pushed around the sloughs looking for frogs and pollywogs. We'd try to sneak up on ducks but we weren't very successful. We built our rafts out of boards and any 2 x 4s we found lying around. We'd get the hammer and nails and nail it together. Sometimes the raft was just a bunch of sticks that we'd lay across poles and then somehow bind them together. We were always going down little creeks or around sloughs on these homemade rafts. I almost drowned one time when I fell in, but our dog pulled me out.

We were free to roam. We could go into the bush and pick seneca root [snakeroot], play hide-and-go-seek, or look for birds' nests. In the summertime we'd hunt for crows' nests because we got a bounty of a cent or so for each egg we found and destroyed. We also collected gopher tails because we got a penny or half a penny for every tail we got. We'd chase the gophers, they'd dash down their holes, and we'd try to dig them out, but we never had much success. We also trapped them, and this worked best.

There were always all kinds of things to discover such as the first flowers in the spring, the first blades of grass, the wonders of nature, and just watching things come up. I remember the birds singing, the way they built their nests and how busy they were feeding their babies. If you stayed still so they didn't detect you, you could watch them feeding their young. I remember seeing and chasing my first jackrabbit and thinking I was going to catch it. I did a lot of running but I never caught the jackrabbit. I enjoyed the freedom of watching things grow and of exploring new things such as new plants and flowers and animals. I remember the robins, the orioles, and the whiskey jacks, and I loved the ducks and geese—to watch them go south in the fall and return in the spring. There was sort of a competition among us kids as to who saw the first robin or the first flock of geese returning.

Dad taught me my directions when I was about four. He would take me out with him to hunt the horses and cattle, and he would tell me he was lost and for me to take him home. He showed me which side of the trees the moss grew on and all the different signs in nature that would show me my directions. To make sure I had a good sense of direction he'd turn me around and around and then I'd have to tell him the directions. When I got older this training served me well. Now I am like a cat, I don't get lost. I think these things helped and I think such training is good for kids. It not only helps in the country, but also in the city to get around without getting lost. He taught me where the sun would be at different times of the day and how to tell time by the sun.

Catalogues were very important. It was great entertainment looking at the things you would like to buy. There were lots of dreams in there. Also, we saw the latest styles and fashions. We'd pick out things that we'd like for Christmas, but we might not get them. One year I got Snakes and Ladders, and another year I got an Eaton's Beauty Doll. I think that came from my aunt. When the catalogue was outdated it went out to the out-house and served another purpose, or else it was used for cutouts and making paper airplanes and paper dolls.

We cut out pictures from newspapers and magazines and made scrap books with them. I made lots of scrap books of families or sometimes households. I still have a scrap book of bird pictures that came on cards in some kind of tea. And another, I think was flowers. We listened to the Lone Ranger, Gang Busters, the Green Hornet, Superman, and Fibber McGee and his closet. We had a battery radio, and the time was limited that you could listen as it was kept for news. I was seven or eight when I first heard a radio and eight when I first saw a telephone.

My brother had a .22 and he used to go hunting. About all he was allowed to hunt were rabbits. At certain times of the year there were lots of rabbits, and during the war rabbit skins were worth nine, ten, or fifteen cents apiece. My brother would shoot, skin, stretch, dry and sell the hides. (The hides were used to line airmen's helmets and jackets.) My brother could skin a rabbit a minute.

I could shoot a gun, and my brother and I used to shoot partridges. I used to trap, but I didn't know how to skin rabbits or I was too slow at it, so I paid my brother one cent to skin each rabbit. We made a little extra spending money that way. I don't know of any other girls that trapped, but I did because I wanted the money. We had an old well that wasn't being used so we'd put brush across it with a little bit of hay on top. We fixed it so if rabbits went there to eat the hay they'd fall into the well. We could go down there and get them. We also used snares, and we shot them. I would go out and look at my trapline every morning before I went to school. Then I'd check it again at night. I did that a couple of winters when I was 12 or 13 and the price of hides was good. After that we moved to B.C.

We always had real good Christmas concerts at our school. It seemed the teacher put in a couple of months preparing us for the Christmas concert. It was quite a big deal. The whole community came with their sleighs. The night of the concert everybody used to dress up in their Sunday best. The horses were decked up with their harness bells, and as we drove to the concert the bells were jingling. Of course, after the concert Santa Claus came with a gift for everybody. It was such a fun time with real community spirit. Generally cakes and tea were served after the concert, but we kids were generally so busy playing with our gifts and our bags of candy and oranges, that we weren't paying much attention to what the adults did. We always had cake, and we'd never miss a piece of cake or cookies.

There were community picnics held at the end of the school year. It was a special thing to go to a picnic and have an ice cream cone. There were races, high jumping, and baseball games. I always went in the races because first prize was generally a nickel and that would buy an ice cream cone. And there were community ball games with the men playing and everyone else watching.

Children were usually included in social activities. There'd be "get togethers" and somebody played the violin, and somebody else played the mouth organ, or maybe the spoons. People took turns getting up to do something to entertain such as a fancy dance step, or singing, or reciting poetry. I learned to dance as a five- or six-year-old kid. Daddy loved to dance. He'd dance round the room and with us in his arms. When we got big enough we'd stand on his feet as he danced, and then on our own feet. I learned all the old fashioned steps, at least what are old fashioned now.

The most pleasant part of childhood was the long lazy days when, as long as my chores were done, I could do what I wanted. In the summer time, it might be just lying on the grass and looking at the sky, watching the clouds go by and daydreaming. Or it might be two or three or four of us kids lying on our tummies and just talking or day dreaming or planning what we were going to do when we grew up. But I did not do what I planned to do when I was young because my plans were very small. Sometimes I think I'd like to go back to those days. I liked that pioneer life, no worries and no rent to pay. There were lots of hardships, but I have lots of pleasant memories.

Maple Leaf Club. *Family Herald and Weekly Star*
January 13, 1904

A FARMER BOY (14)

Dear Editor and Maple Leaves:

I enjoy the members' letters very much, especially those from the "Wild West." I have an uncle living near Winnipeg (whom I was named after). My father and sister were out to see them a year ago, and last fall my brother went out for a month and a half. I would like to go, but they tell me I am too small. Don't you think, Mr. Editor, that the baby of the family is always small longer than the older ones? But I am not going to complain at Christmas time.

We had an entertainment at our school on the evening of the 22nd, the last day of school. I went around to all the people in the section, and asked them to subscribe something towards getting a present for the teacher, of whom we think very much. I collected nearly three dollars.

A neighbour living near, had a little English boy from the Hamilton House and report had it that he abused him dreadfully, and made him sleep in the barn. Consequently his hands and feet were frozen. One night last week he followed me home from school, and was so very hungry, and could scarcely walk that my father could not turn him out. So he wrote to the home, telling the manager what a state the poor little fellow was in, and they came and took him away. Do you think, Mr. Editor, my father did right in writing to the home. He was a little orphan, and I felt sorry for him, so did not send him back, when he said he was going home with me. The man says I coaxed him home, but I didn't and he is very cross over it.

I was one of four boys that acted as pallbearers for a little girl, five years old, that died of erysipelas last week. She, with her two little brothers, younger than herself, and father and mother came home from Alberta a month or so ago, to spend the winter with her mother's parents and this little one was called home. Her parents were reconciled, and said "God's will be done, and it is best."

I think as Apple Blossom does that the most interesting letters are those in which members describe their homes. In my next I will tell you of my home, my brothers and sisters, and my work at home and at school, and last, but not least, my pets, especially the two dogs. I think I have done very well, as far as quantity goes, but how about quality? So will close, wishing all a Happy New year.

WE ALWAYS FOUND SOMETHING TO DO

When R.B. (Bert) Green was growing up in Newfoundland, amenities were few, services were limited, and life was hard, but children still found time to play.

I am 87 years old, and am thinking about my life when I was growing up in a Newfoundland fishing village.

We were let out of school at 4 p.m. It was then my job to chop off, or saw off, the wood, as our house was heated completely by wood stoves. I did the chopping or sawing, and my two sisters — a little younger than I — carried the wood into the house until the wood-box by the stove was piled high with it. It was also my task to bring buckets of water from the nearby brook and fill the water barrel in the porch.

If there was any time left between then and the evening meal, we'd go, in winter, coasting out on the hill, or skating on the nearby frozen marsh, or, in spring and fall, play outdoor games with neighbouring children, such as "Hide and Go Seek," or "Rounders" or other games of our own invention.

In the evenings our time was occupied until bed time, by doing our school homework, and we had lots of it, such as going through our reading lesson, learning spelling, and a section known as "useful knowledge," perhaps memorizing some verses of a poem, and even do an essay. After I was about ten, I had a book on hand to read after the lessons were done, eg, a Horatio Alger—and soon graduated to Zane Grey.

Sometimes, of course, we got our parents or grand-parents (who lived with us) to tell us stories of their boyhood and girlhood.

Some of these activities were carried over into Saturdays also. In early September we could go "in over the hills" (crown-land outside the village) and pick berries. The boys often went into the woods snaring rabbits, or just for a ramble. The girls were somewhat more restricted than the boys, as they had to assist with the household chores—cleaning the floors, peeling the potatoes, etc. On one occasion when I was about ten I laid aside my masculine dignity and volunteered to help my two sisters scrub the kitchen floor. They were puzzled to know what had "come over" their brother, but readily accepted the offer, and it has remained the never-to-be-forgotten event.

In spring the rabbit catching was replaced by trouting in the nearby streams and small lakes. This, of course, was also a male activity, although on one occasion I took my little sister (ten years my junior) along with me and taught her how to fish for trout. She caught twelve, while I caught six!

In summer also we still went trouting—and swimming and berry picking, and occasionally played the outdoor games mentioned above. We also helped our parents in their regular work. They were sea-fishermen, and the boys took part in catching the fish and in the process of "curing the fish," that is, salting it and afterwards washing it and drying it on raised platforms known as "flakes." In the hay-making season all the children took part in spreading the grass that had been cut with a scythe, tossing it over to dry, and then finally each taking his little bundle into the hay-house.

I think perhaps this gives it a fairly good coverage. It was a far more healthy exercise than lying on the living room floor and watching TV. No doubt the TV can be educational also, but our activity was also educational — in the practical things of life.

I WAS INTO EVERYTHING WHEN IT CAME TO SPORTS

Athletics was the focus of Earl Sherman's boyhood, a focus sustained by his own desire and his father's support.

We used to collect bird's eggs. Three of my chums and I would to go out to the country to collect birds' eggs. One of the boys lived on a farm on the outskirts of town and we kept our quite large collection of birds' eggs in his barn loft. My brother Jack (he died when he was only fifteen years old) would climb up the tree and get the eggs out of the nests. He couldn't bring them down without smashing them so he'd drop them into my hat. (I was the designated catcher.) The other boys carried them.

We used to hunt gophers. We got ten cents for gopher tails. I say ten cents but it might have been five. The farmers wanted to get rid of the gophers, so we used to go out and catch them with a string or drown them out. Then, I have to admit, we'd take the tails off the gophers and let them go again so they'd grow another tail. We just figured we'll get that one again next year. (Just grab a gopher by the tail and give it a jerk and the tail slides right off quite nicely.)

We used to play marbles. One morning I went to Bruderheim School, November 14, 1928 it was, and just after we got inside the school caught fire and burned down. It burned so fast and it was so cold, maybe -30°F, that a good number of children had their ears frozen. But by that afternoon we were able to go in among the ashes and find our desks and get our marbles out of our desks.

In the spring, as soon as the ice was off the lake and the ponds, we'd build rafts and go rafting. We used to go behind the section house and get some old railway ties and put them together into a raft and drag them into the water.

Right beside the station was the old water tower, and in the summer we boys would climb up there. It was just a big tank, maybe 12, 14, maybe 20 feet across. The section foreman pumped water from the Saskatchwan River up into the tank. So he could tell how much water was in the tank there were two big cross bars with a stem that went up through a hole in the top of the tank. So as these crossbars floated — up or down — the height of the stem would show the section foreman how much water was in the tank. We used to climb up and swim in between those cross bars. If my Dad had known we were there we'd have got shot for sure! The water was cold but we had fun swimming in there.

Boys' hockey, Sweetwater School #1156, c. 1938.

I shot a wild goose when I was eleven years old. This goose came down the field over our decoys. My Dad shot once or twice and missed it. I was down a little bit further and shot and knocked it down. He said, "Well, son, I sure scared 'heck' out of that goose so you could get him."

We were a family of seven, and I think because my Dad was athletic he pushed us as far as athletics were concerned. I remember one Christmas Dad and Mother had quite a fight because my Dad had gone into Edmonton and bought us boys new hockey trousers, shin pads, the whole bit, just because he wanted to promote our hockey. Mother said he'd spent too much money on the kids' sports. As I got a little older I was playing relatively good hockey. When one of the nearby town teams was going to play a competitive game against another town team, they'd phone up and ask if I could help reinforce their team. I played centre and I did a little bit of coaching, although there was a coach in town. One brother played defense, a second played goal, and Dad was the referee.

As I said, I was "athletics crazy." Just across from the railway tracks was the sports field. There was a race track there, and before I went to school I'd run around the race track eight times because it was five miles — and then I'd walk to school. I was fortunate because my Dad was a station agent and they needed a clerk to meet two passenger trains — one at eleven o'clock at night and the other at six o'clock in the morning. I made application for the job and I got it when I was only fifteen years old. I'd meet the early morning passenger train, and rather than go back to bed I'd jump on my bicycle, go out to the outskirts of town where there was a small field where the ducks used to come in the morning. I'd shoot five or six ducks, come back home, have a quick breakfast, and then go off to school.

Like all kids, on Saturday we'd get our Saturday nickel. We used to pool our nickels, buy a package of cigarettes, and go climb the trees on the outskirts of town where we would smoke the cigarettes. But that was when I was young. I wanted to be a professional hockey player and my dad told me, "Professional hockey players don't smoke and they don't drink." And I didn't! Not even a drink of beer until I was 24 years old.

SONGS TO SING, GAMES TO PLAY, AND PLACES TO EXPLORE

Peggy Sherman recalls Fort Saskatchewan, Alberta, as a wonderful place in which to grow up.

I had twin sisters who were eight years older than I. Their mother died just after they were born, so my Father married her sister. The four of us were born with just a year and a half between. We admired and looked up to our older sisters, but the four of us were very close and we did a lot of things together. My father died when I was six.

In summer we went on picnics, and it didn't seem to matter where we went as long as we took something to eat. We picked berries. Always on Saturday we picked flowers for the house—tiger lilies, roses, etc., as they came along.

We played soft ball, "work-up" it was called. All you needed was a pitcher, catcher and batter. If there was a fourth you had a fielder. We often played on the corner lot just outside our yard, and you know how noisy we could be. Sunday evenings it used to upset Mother that we were out there making so much noise. She'd say, "Why don't you come in and we'll sing some nice hymns?" She'd play the piano and we'd have some kids come that never came to Sunday School. I remember singing "You in Your Small Corner and I in Mine." And after singing we would always have some cocoa or something.

We played marbles and jacks. Everybody had their tin of marbles, we called them alleys and they were made of glass. And there was hopscotch. We used pretty pieces of broken pottery for our toss for playing hopscotch.

Our house was just on the brow of a hill that went down to the river road and then on down to the river. In winter we had our choice of which of four hills we wanted to slide down. When we didn't want to wait for somebody to came back up with the sleigh, well, my father had a big box of shingles left over from shingling the roof—so we used those shingles to slide on down the hill. We went skating practically every night, home by nine o'clock. We played fox and goose and made angels in the snow.

I played with dolls. I can't remember for how long, but I had one beautiful baby doll that I just adored. We played house a lot too. We'd just take sticks and lay them out on the lawn. On rainy days we'd pull the dining room table apart, but we didn't put in a board. We'd stand up in the space and play store. We played rummy and other kinds of card games, crokinole, snakes and ladders, checkers, and parcheesi. We made our own valentines, and that was always a big deal. We read a lot. When we went home for lunch we'd read until the food was on the table. We were usually given books as Christmas and birthday presents.

While my Father was still living, (he died when I was six) we used to go stay in a cabin at Seba Beach. Father drove us out and he'd just come out on weekends. We wore our bathing suits practically all day, swimming, playing on the beach, and fooling around. After supper Mother would take us for a walk away around and up through the town. We took our nickel with us because there was a store that sold cent candy.

My grandparents lived a mile from Fort Saskatchewan, and I remember as a little girl walking out along the tracks and picking crocuses along the way. Grandmother thought they were lovely, but I'm sure she would have appreciated them more if I'd picked them longer [with stems] so she could put them in a vase. We learned to ride horseback out there.

There was a path that ran down to a quiet shaded area beside a lovely little creek. It was only about four blocks from our house, a place where a little girl could walk to and be free to wander around and see the flowers. It was always interesting to go there just to look at things growing. There were leeks, and I remember thinking I should pick some of those and take them home to Mother. I used to go there with friends, too, and when the tadpoles were just coming out we'd get some in jars and take them to school to show the teacher. It was my older sisters who were instrumental in making me aware of these sorts of things. They would take us picking flowers and looking for different things—the Lady Slippers down in the woods. We weren't aware of it then, but looking back we now realize how wonderful it was to have all that freedom.

WHEN OUR PARENTS WERE AWAY

Reprinted with permission from Rex G. Krepps, *As Sparks Fly Upward* (Cloverdale, BC: Friesen, 1989).

The six Krepps children, all born within a seven-year period, could always entertain themselves, and an appreciative audience only added to the fun.

Aileen, being the eldest child of the family, had the awesome responsibility of keeping the younger children in line, when our parents were absent from the farm for any length of time. It was then that we were at our best as actors, actresses or musicians. Our parents were barely out of the yard before the show began. Our barn had a fairly flat roof, a splendid place for a stage to put on a show for our aunt and our cousins. We needed an orchestra; so we dragged up the old wash tub to be used as a drum, the boiler and its lid to be used as a viola, and the plunger used as a fine violin. Our imagination appeared to know no limits; we became a famous orchestra! We sang and did some sort of an imitation of a dance. A sugar water mixture was made for a beverage, and poured into bottles. We were well away! Was this the original barn dance? If it was not the first, it was surely one of the most unique.

The barn dance and orchestra having retired, we had to think of something else to do. For excitement the dog was sent to chase the horses in the pasture, just to see them run. That was short lived though, for a neighbour came by and threatened to tell our parents what we were doing, unless we immediately called off the dog from chasing the horses. We promised, and ceased that form of entertainment.

What was to be done next? Should we have a rodeo? Fine! The calves were in a stall and the pigs were in the pen. What else could a person ask for?

It was great fun to come out of the barn door with a whoop and a holler, the calves pitching and bucking to the best of their ability. We stayed on their backs for three, maybe four jumps, then landed in the manure in the corral. Frank and I took turns riding the calves. We were considered cowboys. The girls did not care to ride those calves, but they happily cheered us on, like good fellows would! It was now time for the pigs to get their run around. Now, a pig is not exactly an easy animal to ride, having nothing to hang on to, and jumping side-ways as they most often did. The trick was to see who could stay on the back of the pig the longest. No one stayed on very long, for with a grumph, and a grunt and a squeal, the pig quickly circled and left us in a heap after a couple of jumps.

"Rex, you see that spotted pig, there?" pointed out Donnie. "Can you ride him?" He asked in a daring way.

"You bet I can; you just bet your life I can," boasted Rex.

"You head him off to the right, " shouted Rex to Doris. "You head him off yourself," hollered Doris in reply. "That pig is crazy, and I'm not. Do you own dirty work." she declared.

The pig was eventually boxed in a corner. Frank waved his hands to make sure the pig was going to put on a good enough show. "Garr-un-m-ph, whoosh whoosh," said the spotted pig, as Rex bounced gleefully on his back. The glee was short lived. George and Lottie Krepps had finished their shopping early, and returned home to the scene of wash tubs, boilers, plungers, and bottles on the barn roof, and of the boys riding the pigs in the pig pen. That was the last straw. Could those children never behave like other nicely behaved children, reading books and behaving themselves in an acceptable way, when the parents were away? It did not appear they would do so willingly. Perhaps they needed a little encouragement, the feel of a razor strap across their behinds. We got it, all six of us. We stoically took our medicine. The rodeo had been a marvelous event, the strapping was worth it all. Besides that, we had the audience of our aunt and cousins. It was evident that our cowboy skills were not honed to perfection, but that would come in time, could it not? Only time would tell.

GROWING UP IN NORTH-CENTRAL BRITISH COLUMBIA

Dick Saunders and his younger brother, Bob, spent much of their time out-of-doors.

My younger brother, Bob, and I grew up in the Prince George area where my father was employed by the C.N. Railway as a "Car Knocker." Dad's responsibilities were repairing, servicing, and inspecting all parts of the train (except the locomotive) for mechanical defects before the train was allowed to proceed.

You asked me to think about the toys I played with when I was young. I recall that in preschool days our toys were not lavish. We had a little red wagon with black rubber tires, and a sled with steel runners. These were standard children's toys. The wagons were made of varnished wood, and usually had red lettering and ornamental designs painted on them. We played marbles too — much to our mother's chagrin as she had to deal with our dirty knees, and worse, sometimes damaged trousers and shoes.

Dad was pretty handy with a hammer and anything he built was rock solid. Among our toys was a wooden block about six to eight inches in diameter, a small hammer, and ready access to a tin can where nails were kept. The blocks were usually small round chunks of firewood, a section cut from the trunk of a tree with an exposed end grain that made for easy driving of nails. As small children, myself first, and then five or so years later, my brother and I together, happily banged nails into wooden blocks. Some of the wooden blocks were pretty well filled up with nails on both ends when we finished with them. By the time we were old enough to be of significant help to Dad with his projects, we had learned useful skills, i.e. how to use a hammer and not mash our thumbs or fingers with a poorly aimed blow!

I remember small wooden tops, and one Christmas we got a metal top that made music. You pumped the central shaft up and down to get it going, and then it played as it spun. I remember Erector Sets, Meccano Sets (they came along when I was quite a bit older), "Pick up Sticks," a ping-pong bat with a captive rubber ball on an elastic string, yo-yos and paper airplanes. There were also

Snakes and Ladders, Checkers, and later on there was Cribbage. We usually had a sponge rubber ball for playing catch, or for playing "fetch" with our dog. "Tuffy" was a cocker spaniel, a hunting dog, and he would retrieve game for us. He would search diligently for an old leather glove when we threw it for him. We often threw a glove into the potato patch without letting him see it, and he would never fail to locate it and bring it back to us.

My brother reminded me that we constructed airplanes from balsa wood kits. The shape of the body, wings and tail were stamped on thin sheets of balsa wood. You cut along the lines with a sharp knife, inserted the wings into the body, installed a balancing weight to make it fly right, and then threw it around the house or out-of-doors if weather permitted. Later on I recall we built more elaborate model airplanes from kits, and they were often powered by twisted elastic bands.

We didn't play softball until we were fairly well along in elementary school. We played a lot of "catch," sometimes just my brother and myself, and sometimes four or five of us would play soft ball—all you really needed was a catcher, a pitcher, a batter, and perhaps someone at first base. You could add other players as they arrived on the scene. We didn't have organized leagues, or referees, or anything like that. I don't recall much enthusiasm for organized team sports among railway people—their irregular work hours and the necessity of earning a living seemed to discourage their participation. There was, however, good fishing and hunting in season, where you could have an enjoyable time and a treat of fish or game if you were successful.

I recall snowball fights at noon hour during school days when the snow conditions were right. Usually it was a few big "high school kids" versus a horde of kids from Grades five, six, and seven. Nobody ever won those snowballs fights as far as I can remember, but there was lots of yelling and running. We slid down a hill near our home on sleds with steel runners. Later, when we were bigger and owned skis we did a bit of cross country skiing at Moore's Meadow, which was about a mile from home. In my memory winter lasted a long time.

Our friend Phillip Jones, his brother Owen and sister Betty, were friends of ours, and Bob and I often went to their place to play. Their back yard was a fascinating place. During construction of the C.N. Railway, contractors used small narrow gauge locomotives, tiny dump cars and small flat cars to carry rails, ties and other supplies to work crews. After the standard gauge tracks were laid the narrow gauge locomotive became surplus. Mr. Jones obtained one of these locomotives. He removed the boiler and installed it in his house to operate his hot water/steam heating system. The rest of the cab was relegated to the back yard where it became a grand play area for us kids.

RATTLES AND STEADIES: MEMOIRS OF A GANDER RIVER MAN

Gary L. Saunders, *Rattles and Steadies: Memories of a Gander River Man* (St. John's: Breakwater Books, 1986). Published with permission of Breakwater. Copyright the author.

The call of the sea and the desire to sail can be very strong. Gary L. Saunders was age six when he went sailing in a wooden packing box.

Climbing aboard, and using a piece of mill edging—what we call crib—for a pole, I pushed out into the current. The brook was in spring flood and top high, and the current was stronger than I bargained for. Pretty soon I lost bottom. Halfway across the brook—which at that point wasn't much over thirty feet—the tide took me and my box and away we went, out past the lumber piles, past the big rock with the ringbolt where the log boom was chained, and on out into the main channel of the bay. By this time the box had settled in the water, which was up to my knees and bitter cold. If I moved at all she would list, which would send me scrambling to the high side, which would only make it list again. It was Uncle John Gillingham heard my screams as he rowed back from tending salmon nets at Sandy Cove on the south side. He took me aboard his punt, wrapped me in his big sweater and rowed me home.

I CAN'T RECALL A DULL MOMENT

Judy Wells, daughter of R.B. Green, lived her first eleven years at Gander Falls, Newfoundland. There is an interesting contrast between the childhood years of father and daughter.

Television wasn't in my vocabulary until my family moved to Ontario in 1955 and we would be invited to neighbours' homes to see "I Love Lucy" on Monday nights and cartoons and westerns on Saturday mornings.

I can't recall a dull moment "before television." Time was filled with reading (Bobbsey Twins, Nancy Drew, and the Hardy Boys, etc.) long after lights out by use of a flashlight under the covers. Other indoor activities might be making crafts, using suggestions from mom's old teacher's manual, playing madeup paper games, such as Consequences (several people sat around the table, each with a sheet of paper and pencil. First, one would write an adjective and then fold the paper over so no one could read the word and then pass the paper to the next person who would write the name of a well-known male, either famous, a family member, or a local, fold and pass along. Next, another adjective—a well known female name [oh yes, one should write the word met after the male name to make the story flow], then the setting where they met—what he said, what she said, and the final outcome. Eight times the paper would be passed and then opened.) What laughter would erupt when these mixed up stories were read out! My sisters and I so enjoyed this game that we played it over and over with our own families—especially when camping.

We also loved to get old catalogues and cut out people and make up stories using the cutouts. Often we would cut out other outfits from the catalogue and lick them to have them stick on the originals. What a treat it would be to be given a real cutout book where the outfits could be put on the figures with little tabs instead of having to lick them to stick!

I could go on and on about rainy day activities, playing house or doctor (we never played school as we had enough of that from 9-4), experimenting with the short wave band on our radio, or getting a blanket and sliding down the wooden staircase.

We loved playing outdoors and spent hours in our yard with neighbours involved in games such as hide and seek, statues (where a leader would fling the rest, one at a time, with all his strength in a circle until they broke off and landed in some strange position which they would maintain until the leader chose the best to be the next leader), or just climbing on dad's pile of birch logs not yet sawed up for fuel.

I once found a lovely soft wide round chunk of wood and spent a most enjoyable morning driving in nails in the warm sunshine. How was I to know that it was my father's chopping block!

Our favourite pastime was to make up plays and perform them for the rest of the neighbourhood children, 1 cent admittance. An old unused hen house in the yard made a grand theatre.

I spent hours on my bicycle, which I still have, going all over town, even to the next town, 10 miles away, with friends.

On hot summer days we set up a Freshie stand and sold drinks to the thirsty mill workers as they walked home from work. We had lots of family picnics just out of town by the big Exploits River where we could see logs floating by on their way to the paper mill in town. Dad made many attempts to try to teach us to swim.

In winter we did everything we could to snow — shovelled paths for 10 cents, made tunnels, igloos, snow people, and horses, spent hours on our wooden sleighs with iron runners, and even ate the odd mouthful.

We would collect the neighbours' Christmas trees and make a teepee by tying them together at the top and putting branches on the floor. What a cosy hut this made.

Summer holidays were always something to look forward to. Mostly, we put our car on the train (the highway didn't go all the way) and went to our grandparents' homes in the New-foundland outports. There was always a little boat which my sisters and our cousins were allowed to row in the cove. Often, the fishermen would let me go out squid-jigging with them in the early evening. One had to have a strong stomach for this activity as squid juice has an unpleasant odor. But it was worth it to be able to be in an open boat on the ocean waves.

All year round there were community and church activities to capture our interest—Brownies, concerts, choir, local baseball and hockey games, a Labour Day parade where I could decorate my bicycle and enter the parade, a skating carnival with prizes to be won for the best costumes.

To this day, I could live without television. The childhood lessons of self-entertainment have served me well.

THE EFFECTS OF A DISTANT WAR

Paul Barker recalls his Nova Scotia childhood.

In 1942 my parents moved to Yarmouth, N.S. It was during the war years and at that time Yarmouth was an exciting place. Members of the armed services were a common sight as well as planes, jeeps and other war vehicles. We were constantly glued to the radio to hear what was happening overseas. It was during that period that I became interested in radio episodes such as Captain Midnight, Jack Armstrong and the Lone Ranger. My parents were very fond of reading and every night before my brother and I went to bed they would read to us. As time went on I embraced this love of reading and I became an avid reader.

The war, radio programs and reading had a great effect on what I played. I possessed a good imagination and I would act out a lot of the things that I heard or read about. With my friends we played war games with our toy guns and grenades. I remember putting a wooden box on my wagon and on top of this a bushel basket. With a broom handle sticking out of the basket I had an army tank. The cover of a bushel basket was a shield and with a wooden sword I was a knight. I made a bow and some arrows and I became Robin Hood. I was able to fashion a cave in the back yard for the enactment of Aladdin and Ali Baba. My grandparents gave me an old phonograph and some records and with this I created a radio station. For Xmas one year I received a coping saw and a vise and I was thus enabled to create a lot of the props I needed.

Shortly after we moved to Yarmouth, I started school. During the next few years I was not particularly interested in girls and so the games I participated in tended to be with other guys and to be quite active. We played tag, ball tag, frozen tag, hide-and-seek, and Simon says. One game that I was fond of was kick-the-can. In the spring we flew kites and often we would drop toy parachutes and toss gliders off the fire escape of our school.

In the evenings, especially in winter, we as a family used to play card games, go-fish, Lost Heir, Old Maid, Parcheesi, checkers and crokinole to name but a few. I remember buying my mother a game of bingo for Xmas one year because I was particularly interested in it.

Like the other boys in the neighbourhood, I was a collector of everything, rocks, shells, marbles, comics and stamps.

My mother's parents had a farm in New Hampshire and one month of each year was spent there. I collected eggs, picked berries and vegetables, helped with haying and did other chores. As part of the farm was heavily wooded I would go for long hikes with the dog. I enjoyed the association with my grandfather who had a wide variety of interests and readily shared them, especially his love of nature. During the war years we had no car so travel to New Hampshire and elsewhere was done by train.

Dad was fascinated with trains and this fascination rubbed off on my brother and I. Each day the train from Halifax would come into Yarmouth. After the passengers were let off, the engine would be uncoupled from the rest of the cars and it would back up to a place outside of town where there was a "Y." It would turn around and thus would be facing in the right direction when it made its trip to Halifax the next day. The engine would pass close to our house and occasionally the engineer who was dad's cousin would stop and let dad, my brother and I on as the engine went to turn around. Later on my brother and I received a Lionel train set that had been our uncle's. Needless to say we had hours of fun with this set.

What I have described in detail is that period of my life between the age of six and eleven. In 1947 we moved to Stirling, Ontario, and there things changed dramatically. I became very involved in team sports, softball, soccer, football and hockey.

MY GAMES PARALLEL MY LIFE

By the mid-1950s television was available in many areas of Canada, but not in Ocean Falls, British Columbia. Kim Gosse Hilliard recalls her busy childhood.

When asked to reflect on childhood play without television and what influenced me, what activities I pursued and what props I used, I had a lot of fun making associations with my present activities and the person I am today. I am not clear as to what play I participated in for the first five years of my life. Photos show me with a doll house, tea set, and the usual female toys. I do remember coming inside from play to listen to the radio at specific times, the most memorable show being "Fibber McGee & Molly" and their infamous closet.

My most prominent recollections begin in 1956 when my family moved to Ocean Falls, B.C. I started grade one that year, my first experience with the school system and peers. Winters were long and dark and one of my favorite times was in the evening when my mom would read to me and my brother and sister. She introduced me to Heidi and the Bobbsey twins and the excitement of mysteries. I later loved to read Nancy Drew on my own. Inside I could roller skate in the basement on the cement floor. I like to color and always played with dolls, particularly baby dolls. Outside I rode my bike, played with friends and had free rein of the open spaces as Ocean Falls was a very close knit community and no one worried about "strangers." My friends and I would play "dress up" with whatever materials we could find. We wandered along the beach, playing in the piled up drift wood and hiked down the only road to "Twin Lakes," playing in the huge blast rock on the side of the road. One theme was always prominent, I like to "play house" and I recall always wanting to be the mother. I would set out designating cubbyholes as the kitchen, living room and bedrooms. I cooked with mud and whatever other delicacies I could find in whatever containers I could scrounge up. Alone or with friends, play always consisted of makeshift material created from things from home or found outside and on the beach. Toys were very few and very basic. We always had books and made use of the library. Roller skates and bikes, coloring books and crayons, a baby doll, a teddy bear and the coveted doll buggy I received when I was seven. These were the only commercial props, the rest was imagination.

"The good old days," 1952. Keith and Kim Gosse, Prince George farm.

At the age of eight to twelve years, my family moved to Bellingham, Washington. Quite a contrast to the remote and isolated town of Ocean Falls. Outside play was restricted to the fenced back yard or roller skating or bike riding around the block on the sidewalk. I read a lot and discovered sewing. I liked to create clothes for my life size baby doll. My sister and I played "office" at the piano bench with the old invoices my father brought home from work. Television was available in Bellingham, but not a big part of our life. I remember the Saturday my father brought home a little black and white TV and the first show I saw was "Heckle and Jeckle" cartoons. Sunday nights the family would watch "Ed Sullivan" or "Red Skelton." Saturdays we were allowed limited cartoons, half an hour or so and then the TV was turned off. Even though the television was not a regular influence in our home, its influence was still felt by my peers and it stimulated their need to "have the right stuff" for whatever fad was in at the time. Commercialism had its foot hold.

At age twelve my family moved back to Ocean Falls. Reading and listening to the radio were big on the entertainment list. Socializing in any form was most important. Puberty was on the horizon and maintaining the perfect French roll and getting as much mirror time in the bathroom as possible was a high priority. Child play was over.

Upon reflection of the activities I enjoyed as a child and the creative process I engaged, I found it interesting how much they paralleled the choices I made as an adult, the path I have followed and the activities I have enjoyed. It may well answer the age old question, "Who am I?"

Playing Is Playing
When Shared

MAPLE LEAF CLUB PICNIC

Maple Leaf Club, *Family Herald and Weekly Star*
August 21, 1901

Ethel Swan (10)
The Willows
Austin, Manitoba

On the 24th of May I gave a party to the Maple Leaf Club, of which I am president. "What club? Ours?" Why, no; the club of Austin, which is formed of girls and boys from four to fourteen years, and the ones who gave a concert for the Indian Hospital on the 13th of June.

As we live in the country, and most of the club live in town, my father drove a waggon and team in for them. As soon as they got here we practiced our pieces for the concert. Then we played croquet, baseball, red line and drop the handkerchief. About four o'clock we had ice cream, and then played hide-and-seek till tea time which we had on the lawn. Then two girls and myself washed the dishes, and then played cricket. But I saw that the little ones had nothing to play, so I played with them, and we had some fine games of "Here we come gathering nuts in May," "Farmer in the dell," "Here comes one King," and "All around the village." Then came more practice and some more ice cream, and the waggon was ready to take them home. I went too, and we all had flags to wave, so we shouted and sang all the way to town. We ended our day by singing "The Maple Leaf" and giving three cheers for the "Maple Leaf Club."

STRANGE BEDFELLOWS

Maple Leaf Club, *Family Herald and Weekly Star*
September 21, 1904

CHICK
Assiniboia

It is quite a long time since I wrote last. I am away for my summer holidays now, and am having a very good time. I am visiting my uncle and aunt. My uncle is an inspector of Indian agencies and we are right on a reserve.

Until a short time ago there were 15 of us in the house, as my aunt had quite a lot of visitors. But at present there are only seven of us and we feel rather lonely. My uncle is away now inspecting an agency about 60 miles off.

For quite a long time we were sleeping in tents. There were two tents up and five of us girls slept in one and two boys in the other. We had a great deal of fun playing tricks on each other, and one night we were up till two in the morning. Towards the last our enjoyment was spoiled by lizards, which became a a perfect pest. When my uncle went away he took the tents with him, and so our good times in them ended. But three of us girls, upon sleeping one night in the house, resolved that some way or other we would manage to sleep outside again. So next day we fixed up blankets around part of the verandah and made our beds in this bedroom. The first two nights we enjoyed it splendidly, but the third time, just as we were dropping off to sleep, some one gave a scream. My aunt brought a lamp from the house to see what the matter was. There was a huge lizard crawling just close to our heads. We all retired to the house in a hurry and have slept inside ever since. But we were just speaking the other day about trying it again after putting boards all around the edges of the verandah.

The day after we came here we drove up to the Government ranch. I saw them rounding cattle out of the corral, which was quite a novel sight for me. We camped for our supper, which was the best fun of all.

A couple of weeks ago we drove to Indian Head, a distance of 36 miles. On our return we passed through a small town that had just been started. It was on Sunday, and it did present a most deserted appearance. Three days later they celebrated the arrival of the first passenger train into their town. We attended the celebration. We could not help contrasting the look of the town then with what it had looked like the previous Sunday. We passed an interesting day.

We went in paddling in one of the sloughs yesterday, and had a very good time. We intended going in swimming to-day, but it was too cold. This is the first [day] of shooting and we expect a good dinner tonight.

I will conclude my rather lengthy letter by informing the Editor that as I have written on the typewriter only two or three times before, I hope he will excuse any mistakes there are.

THE KAY CHILDREN

Family Herald and Weekly Star
June 11, 1911

Kathleen and Katy are delighted girls because their little cousin have come from town to spend the summer with them. They are going to take him to a picnic, and will be ready to start, with their baskets, as soon as they get their pretty Summer things on. Katy is very anxious to wear her new habitant hat. Kenneth longs to catch butterflies in his net, and Kathleen, who has a smart new jersey dress, feels a great deal of responsibility about the lunch baskets.

Directions

Paste the figures on thin cardboard, then cut out carefully. For cutting some portions a sharp pointed knife is best. To make the dolls stand paste the turned over end of a narrow strip of stiff paper to the middle of each doll's back. Make the strips long enough to support the figures. The dresses and hats need not be stiffened.

OUR PAPER DOLLS.

THE KAY CHILDREN.

SCOUTS AND SMOKING

Maple Leaf Club, *Family Herald and Weekly Star*
January 10, 1911

A scout does not smoke. Any boy can smoke; it is not such a very wonderful thing to do. But a boy scout will not do it because it is foolish. He knows that when a boy smokes before he is fully grown up it is always sure to make his heart feeble, and the heart is the most important organ in a boy's body. It pumps the blood all over him to form flesh, bones and muscle. If the heart does [not] do its work the body cannot grow to be healthy. It also injures the eyesight and sense of smell.

No boy ever began smoking because he liked it, but generally because either he feared being laughed at as afraid to smoke, or because he thought by smoking he would look like a great man—when all that time he succeeds only in looking silly. So don't be persuaded. Just make up your mind for yourself that as a boy you won't smoke. That will show you to be much more of a man than any going about with a half smoked cigarette tilted between your teeth, your hands in your pocket and your hat on the side of your head. Your chums will respect you the more, and in many cases follow your example.

THE VERY BEST TIME FOR US

Reprinted with permission from Barry Broadfoot, *Memories of Settlers Who Opened the West: The Pioneer Years 1895-1914* (Toronto: Doubleday, 1978).

The school was more than an educational institution; it was also a place where the entire community came together.

Outside in the spring and fall we had a baseball diamond. The school board gave us one ball a year and that had to last. The bat lasted longer than that, of course, but if it broke, you could always go to the poplar bluff by the barn and whittle out another. The bat didn't matter but the ball sure did. Once it started to unravel, somebody would take it home and get their dad to fix it.

For the little kids there were swings. Know what they were? They put up two poles and then a crossbar across the top and they got a lot of old horsecollars, ones that were no good anymore, and they tied them with rope to the crossbar and that was the kids' swings. Pretty good too.

Every year just after school was out we would have a field day. About two days before the big day Mr. Banks and his hired man would come and bring his mower and cut down any grass that had grown too tall and then he'd rake it. The next day the men would come, and in the barn there were several boards and stools and benches and they would set them up outside. Usually in the shade of the schoolhouse or where it was going to be shady about three in the afternoon. Somebody would mark off 50 yards—that was for the racing—and if there was any boards to be fixed up in the backstop, then they were hammered in. That was for the ballgame. That's when we got the new ball. The new ball was brought for the First of July field day and then given to the school for the rest of the year, starting some time in September.

Things started about one in the afternoon, as I recall. Everybody came. The children of the school, of course, and their families and the hired men and bachelors in the district. There were always a lot of them. But we didn't get those that weren't ours. Schools were pretty close together in those days because of the cold and children walking, so each bachelor went to his own school unless he was sweet on the teacher. That often happened.

Things were run by the head of the school district or some important man. I mean he was the one who handed out the prizes. For the children I think a first prize in the three-legged race might be 50 cents to the winners and they split. Twenty-five cents to the winner of the 50-yard dash. They didn't have things like the high jump and the broad jump, as I remember. Mostly running races. There was one that was a lot of fun and everybody played it, and that was the mixed shoe race. Down at one end everybody would take of his shoes and they'd be put together, all mumbledy-jumbledy in a pile. You had to run down and find your own shoes, put them on and run back to the finish line. Egg and spoon race. Blindfolded race. That was funny. And just straight races, of course.

Then everybody would eat. Everybody brought pies and potato salad and cold meat and cookies, tarts, buttered buns with jam, pickles, and you just didn't eat what you'd brought. Everything was put on the table and you ate anything you wanted, and if you wanted more, then you went and got it. Nobody said anything.

Then there was a ball game. Sometimes the bachelors played the married men, or sometimes a team would come from town or the next district and there would be quite a game. We had some darn fine players in those days, fellows who could throw a ball through a hole in a barn from 50 feet or slap that old ball into any part of the field they wanted. Some, I guess, could have gone into Regina or Moose Jaw or down south and played with the big teams there, but they never seemed to. Their speed was just down on the farm.

SCHOOL FIELD DAY

Maple Leaf Club, *Family Herald and Weekly Star*
July 7, 1915

Janet McNab
DAISY
Douglass, Ont.

Dear Maple Leaves:

Will you please let me enter that cozy little corner of yours, the Maple Leaf Club? I am a reader of all letters and enjoy them all very much.

My object in writing is to tell you of the Field Day our school held on the 3rd of June.

Our program was a fine one; it consisted of drills, addresses and also sports. There were two baseball matches, and one basketball and our team came out successful every time.

The day passed too quickly and we were disappointed in not having our sports.

We had a dandy supper which consisted of salads, peas, beans, sandwiches and cakes. When I got home it was eight o'clock. I had a splendid time.

The proceeds went to build a rink on the school play-ground and to beautify the school yard.

SPORTS WERE FINE

Maple Leaf Club, *Family Herald and Weekly Star*
September 15, 1915

Byron Kingsbury
MOOSE HUNTER
Edam, Sask.

Dear Maple Leaves:

A short time ago I went to a picnic with some friends, we drove twenty-two miles with a horse. It was a long and tiresome drive, but the sports were fine,—chiefly horse racing, baseball and football. I liked the baseball best of all. When the sports were over there was a dance. I did not go as I was young, but my friends went. The dance did not finish till nearly daylight, then we started home.

I would like to correspond with Woodchuck; I am ten years old.

WENT TO PICNIC IN AN OX CART

Maple Leaf Club, *Family Herald and Weekly Star*
September 8, 1915

Ellsworth V. Griffin
HACMACTACK
Sable River, Shellburne Co. N.S.
(hope that you enjoyed the picnic. I received so many drawings that I can't remember if yours was amongst them. — Editor.)

Dear Maple Leaves:

I have not written to our club for quite a while. I wrote two letters, but did not see them in print.

We had a picnic on Victoria Day in Granite Village. We went there on the ox-team and had a good time getting back at night. I am going to the Temperance Picnic to be held at Port Clyde this month (August). I was there last year and had a good time.

The blueberries are very plentiful this year; we have quite a number of quarts since they began to ripen.

I sent a drawing, but forgot to send a slip of paper with my parents or persons name so I don't know whether it was all right or not.

GOING TO MAKE A PLAYHOUSE

Maple Leaf Club, *Family Herald and Weekly Star*
June 9, 1915

Margaret Muskett
OLD MOTHER GOOSE
Peerless P.O., Carlstadt, Alta.

Dear Maple Leaves:

Last winter my brothers and my sister and I tunnelled under a big snow drift in our yard. First we made three tunnels, then we joined them and made a nice big room. We went on digging till it was about 20 feet long and 10 feet wide. We had nearly finished it when it started to thaw. We also dug a hole that we are going to make into a playhouse this summer. We made it once before, but a cow walked on the roof and broke it in. It did not hurt the cow, luckily, but it spoilt the roof. We did not have school last winter, so my sister and I did lessons at home. I have three brothers and one sister, two are Maple Leaves. I also know of two other Leaves near here, although we are ten miles from the nearest town. Three years ago the nearest town was forty miles away. I am in sixth grade. I am twelve years old.

BOYS' FARMING CLUB

Boys' and Girls' Clubs, *Grain Growers' Guide*
March 29, 1916

Reggie Meeks (14)
Mannville, Alta.

(Third Prize Letter)

Two years ago the boys in my district started a Boys' Farming club. Each boy was to get an acre from his father and he was to grow a garden and experiment with other things. We were to build a chicken coop and raise some chickens on the acre of land.

We each had a calf and little pig to raise and we could do any other thing we wanted to.

One warm Saturday morning we met by a little bluff to choose our secretary, manager and other officers. We made certain rules that we were to follow. We decided to have a concert to raise money to start our club. On the third of January our concert came off and we earned eighty dollars after we had paid expenses. There were only ten in our club, so we had enough to buy seeds and a little pig for each one, and we had thirty dollars left to give away on prizes when we had our little fair. The farmers supplied us with calves and chickens. Each year we are getting more people to join our club.

FROM SMALL TOWN TO BIG CITY

As Ann Thrasher Rogers discovered, there were differences in the games played in remote settlements and those played in big cities.

Until I was eight years old I lived in Snowshoe, a small settlement which grew up around my father's sawmill on the Fraser River, between McBride and Prince George. There were never more than twenty children attending the one room school, and although we often played with those in our own age group there were some games such as Kick the Can and Anti-I-Over which went better if the whole school participated. The former game was hide and seek with "home free" person being required to kick the can at home base. As I remember the latter game required players on either side of the school equally divided; someone threw the ball over the roof, shouted "anti" etc., and the one catching the ball dashed to the other side, to tag someone, thereby collecting another team member. The game continued until one side was eliminated.

I played hopscotch by the hour with two or three girls my age. We drew the squares on the packed mud of the road outside one girl's home. It was not level but that just made the game more challenging. We redrew the squares so often that they became deeply grooved in the mud. Our "hopscotches" were flat stones, or bits of broken glass or crockery. When I moved to Vancouver in 1942 I discovered just how sophisticated this game could be. Here the players used hopscotches made of multi-coloured beads, threaded in many loops. We envied one girl who had access to her grandmother's attic and the beaded fringes on old lamp shades and evening bags. Trading of these items took place according to a very strict code.

My brother Duncan remembers from Snowshoe days marathon games of hide and seek, played after supper in the late spring and through the summer. We all wore long shirts and pants and kept moving as clouds of mosquitoes followed us. Duncan also remembers that he amused himself for hours throwing rocks at various targets, thereby developing his good pitching arm for baseball, but giving our mother anxious moments— "He's always throwing at something." The Fraser River, rolling with awesome energy past Snowshoe and the sawmill, was a source of fascination to all of us, but especially to Duncan and his pals as they threw their rocks at the moving targets it offered.

My big brother Fred, several years older than I, was always grouped with the adults in my memories of Snowshoe. He spent much of his time around the mill and eventually worked there. He remembers the big flood of 1936 when everything including the schoolhouse was afloat. He and his friend made a raft, and paddled in places where before they had walked. Their raft was narrow enough to sail through the schoolroom door and rescue, at the teacher's request, some books and papers from her desk. My brother and his friend were tickled to find that they could have fun while being of service.

In Snowshoe, where there was only one small store, the Eaton's catalogue provided hours of entertainment. Besides just poring over it and making a wish list, we cut up old issues, furnishing rooms in our scrapbooks and creating families from the figures modelling the clothes.

My sister Judith was only three when we moved from Snowshoe, but even then she could spend hours communing with her family of imaginary playmates. She gave them unusual names and demanded we all treat them with respect. I remember my father patiently holding the back door open while "Mrs. Kickedy" or "Mrs. Blue" came in from whatever adventure Judith had arranged that day.

In Vancouver I discovered bicycling and roller-skating, skipping, and elaborate games played with lacrosse balls. At school long ropes were provided for our skipping activities, and we worked our way through dozens of skipping songs or chants, some of them very topical, about sinking submarines and the boys in blue. Anyone who tripped on the rope had to take one end of it and help turn.

In our neighbourhood in Vancouver we children would gather almost every evening after supper, when the daylight lasted, and play such games as Statues and "Mother May I"? The rules for these escape me now. I remember instead one girl in the group who had a very strict curfew, and when the whistle shrilled from her front porch up the block, she was off, no matter what crucial point we had reached in our game. We were all aware of her anxiety as she sped home.

With the lacrosse balls we played "One, Two Three Alarey O," where you put first one leg and then the other over the ball, clapped your hands behind your back and made other complicated gestures, all the time bouncing this hard rubber ball, which if you fumbled, could escape from you and tear away, rising higher each time it struck the pavement, finally disappearing down the hill or into someone's garden. I soon lost my supply of these aggressive playthings, and others were loath to lend what was a scarce pre-war commodity.

In the midst of all these activities I have described reading took up much of my time. Our mother read to us and taught me to read early, and it has always been one of my greatest pleasures.

CAMP FIRE GIRL

Maple Leaf Club, *Family Herald and Weekly Star*
February 10, 1919

Hattie Morrill (15)
Derby, Ont.

Dear Maple Leaves:

I go to Derby Academy and like it very much. I take domestic science.

I have not seen any letters from the good old "Green Mountain State," Vermont.

I belong to Camp Fire Girls. I am a fire maker now. I have the wood gatherer's ring and also the bracelet.

We go on hikes and have great sport, in winter we go skiing and we always come home tired almost to death.

I would like to correspond with either sex about my own age.

A CHARIVARI

Pathfinders' Page, *Free Press Prairie Farmer*
November 20, 1920

Iola Crouse (11)
Killarney, Man.

Dear Pathfinders:

Not long ago one of our neighbors' daughters got married and a bunch of us gave her a charivari [shivaree]. The groom gave one of the biggest boys $7. The boys gave the girls only 15 cents apiece and kept the rest for themselves. Now, that's just like a boy, isn't it? Last Friday afternoon at school we had a concert after recess. One of my girl chums and I dressed up as ghosts. We both had masks and I had a pair of white gloves. We came in and shook hands with some of the scholars. Then we went out and went over to the old school and gave the class a surprise. It sure was fun. Well, I will close with a riddle.

Q. What can be lengthened by cutting a piece off each end?
A. A trench or ditch.

HOW I HAD FUN AS A KID

*The Moulton children combined Ivy's love of animals with
Jack's mechanical abilities to create their own equipment
and games.*

The year I was born there were very few babies born in our district. I grew up on the farm and my playmates were the farm animals. I always had cats, dogs, horses, and calves with which to play. My only brother is three years older than I. He is very mechanically inclined and works very well with his hands. On the other hand, I am a voracious reader, and animal lover and completely mechanically illiterate. It was once said that the only thing Jack and I have in common is our parents.

My earliest memories are of pretend games I played. I would pretend I was a wild horse and run about, stopping every once in a while to nicker. I got so good at it that sometimes the horses would even answer me.

Jack and I would also play with items we found about the farm. For example, we used old gears from machinery and rolled them along the ground in a corner of the garden, building roads, dugouts, and ponds.

One autumn Dad bought a pony for us. We rode her and drove her. One summer we needed a cart for her, so we took the old harrow cart that had been used on the farm years ago. We adapted it to our use by moving the bars that had held the harrow sections around to the front, and they became the shafts. The shafts were not set solid so we would grab one of the wheels, which were steel, to straighten everything up so the wheels weren't rubbing against the steel shaft.

Later on, after I had started school, Dad bought another pony for us. One summer we harnessed that pair of Shetland ponies to the scuffle cultivator (used by Mom and Dad to work between the rows of potatoes) and worked up part of the garden.

We were doing the summer fallowing, you see. I was the driver and Jack guided the cultivator. One day we hitched the ponies to a four section harrow set and were very upset that Dollie and Babe couldn't pull it. Dad told us that four sections of harrows were meant to be pulled by a team of draft horses. After that we used a single harrow for the ponies. Mother said she had one of her best gardens ever on that plot the following summer, nearly weed free because a weed only had to poke its nose through and we would work up the whole area again.

Ivy and Jack Moulton on their "arse cart."

During the winter we spent quite a bit of time listening to the radio. Some of the shows we followed were Superman, The Lone Ranger, and Fibber McGee and Mollie. Our favorite show was "L" for Lanky. It was the story of a Lancaster bomber's missions over Europe during World War II. On Saturday evenings we listened to Foster Hewitt and Hockey Night in Canada. I remember the night I went to bed in tears. That night Syl Apps went crashing into the goal post and broke his leg. I knew that without Syl Apps the Leafs would not win the Stanley Cup—and they didn't!!!!

At our local one room school we played the usual games, tag, pump-pump-pull-away, softball, and hockey. Everyone played, regardless of age or gender. Sometimes our games were very imaginative and we made up new activities. Once we played "pirate." We brought "treasures" from home and buried them in the spruce shelterbelt that surrounded the grounds. I imagine some of them are still there.

Of course, as a family, we took part in community events. There was the annual school picnic with races and ice cream. We always had an annual Christmas concert. Every student took part and the whole district attended. We often attended the other school concerts in the surrounding districts. Occasionally there were whist drives at the school. Everyone went, regardless of age, to all the community events; grandparents, parents, and children of all ages. As the babies and toddlers tired, they were put to sleep on coats on the cloakroom floors and the evening continued. Babysitters were unheard of as the activities were family oriented.

Looking back I can say that I had a very happy childhood and I wouldn't change the past in any way.

WE HAD FREEDOM GALORE

Shirley Dawn McKim and her siblings roamed, without fear
or censure, the fields, woods, and streams of their community.

I grew up in Brookdale, Nova Scotia, four miles on a gravel road out of Amherst. We didn't have a car or horses or anything, so we seldom went anywhere else besides Brookdale. We were four girls and a boy, Beryl, Larry (Lar), Betts, and then me. It took five years to supply the world with those four children, and five years later Sheila arrived. When we were kids all we saw were our own family and the neighbour kids—there were about seven of them I think—the Millers. Four of us, Betts and me, Joan, and Dot Miller all went around together like one person. We were out together almost every day. We played at our house or we played at their place. Nobody ever looked after us, nobody organized games or came to see we didn't fall out of trees, or off the top beam of the barn, or the roof of the house. We just had freedom galore and nobody checked up on us.

Betts and I played together much of the time, and one of our jobs was to go get the milk from the neighbours. Our dad was a school teacher and all the other people around were on farms. Everyday, after supper, we went down to the Coates to get milk. A quart of milk was four cents, and we got a quart and a pint everyday. Every once in a while we'd get eggs as well, and Mrs. Coates would get a paper bag and take one egg and wrap the egg in a piece of newspaper about 6 x 6 inches. Well, we played store all the time and we sold eggs, and if anybody came by and watched us wrapping up those stones and putting them in a sack they must have wondered what we were doing — we were selling eggs.

We made mud cakes, mud pies, and mud cookies, and we always seemed to sell them, we were great entrepreneurs. We made cardboard money the size of a quarter, a nickel, a dime, and a penny and we'd dole it all out. I guess that is where we learned to reckon. Sometimes we just had an imaginary person running the store and we were both buyers. But once in a while one of us would be the store keeper. Most of the time just Betts and I played store as Sheila was too young to do all of that stuff, but she'd eat the cookies even if they were mud.

We'd play store and we'd also play school. Boy, we were the meanest teachers you ever saw. We'd always take the ruler to somebody, yet in our school nobody ever got a licking. We also played Sunday school, everyone in that community went to Sunday school. Betts and I would arrange our chairs in little rows like pews, and we'd stand on top of the piano for the choir. Mom never told us to get off the piano, she never interfered with our sermons or our Bible readings, or whatever. I don't know that we could actually read, but we played church for hours.

In the summertime we'd play outdoors. We'd put a quilt down and that was our house. Betts was the mother and I was the father because I couldn't be bothered sitting down and changing clothes on baby dolls — it didn't interest me at all. So I would be Uncle By and she would be Aunt Grace. I'd say, "Well Grace, I'm going out and work in the backyard." And I'd go out into the backyard and I'd hoe, make drains and little rivers and streams, and I'd rake. Then I'd come back in and she'd have supper ready by then—sandwiches. They were about the size of your thumb nail. And I had to take two bites out of it because that was how is was done. Two bites out of a thing like that! In order to keep peace in the family I did it. And she had these little dishes, and the toy cups filled with water. (Real china cups, Santa Claus gave them to us.) We'd play house for hours. Betts wasn't really that strong, she had pneumonia two or three times before she went to school so she was very frail. She was content to sit there and do doll clothes and make sandwiches. It worked fine as I was kind of robust and climbed trees and showed off. I was happy with my role and she was happy with hers.

We were allowed to do anything we wanted. We had about 90 acres of woods and I bet we knew every tree in that place. We'd go for hours in the woods and pick berries, that was the main thing we went out for—blueberries by the zillions and quite a few raspberry patches. A brook went through our place, and we cleared a place not quite as big as this room—we called it our swimming hole. The water was up to about our knees, and that's a child's knees. We used to fish for shiners with a straight pin on a piece of string.

As we tramped about we came to know every plant and every tree, where the birds' nests were, which things were safe to eat and which were not—and we ate most everything. Dad taught school and he was away during the week. On Sunday we'd go for a walk in the woods with Dad. I guess he was looking where he would cut the next tree for wood burning. He'd tell us everything that was going on, which roots we could eat or which berries to avoid. We'd walk around for an hour and a half, I guess.

There were no organizations for children except the Junior Red Cross which met every Friday afternoon for perhaps an hour. We had a business meeting and it was run really well. The teacher taught us how to run a business meeting and things like how to put on a sling to rest your arm or bandage your leg. Sometimes we raised money for something. I remember one time we raised money for a wheel chair coach [bus]. We drew pictures of the coach and we sold them as greeting cards for this coach in Halifax. We had programs, too, and that day we could play games in the school. The program was run by the teacher or a committee that was supposed to be looking after entertainment. We knit squares for an afghan. All you did was cast on about 35 stitches, knit back and forth until you ended up with a block that was maybe 6 inches square. Then you'd do another one, and somebody sewed that all together. I think everybody in the school knit during wartime.

Children playing on swings, c. 1900 (Vancouver Public Library, Special Collections [8058]).

I belonged to the Maple Leaf Club in the *Family Herald and Weekly Sta*r. I was seven years old when I joined. We all had pen names and mine was Grasshopper. I said that I liked to run and play in the fields and trees and grasses and to hop around and never be still. And I called myself Grasshopper. In the publication they drew a picture of a grasshopper beside my letter. I thought that was great and I coloured that thing. I bet I could still find it among my treasures. I was seven years old and I had a whole lot of correspondents, five or six girls and a boy in Hawaii, that I wrote to faithfully for several years. I never met any of them, but we had a correspondence going. We exchanged pictures. And one of my hobbies was pressing flowers, and I'd press them and write down where I picked them and what the name of them was and everything. And I'd send some to my penpals, and I got things back. I got a jigsaw puzzle one time from a girl in England. But I can't imagine any seven year old now writing letters and having them sent in the mail. That was fun, the stamp was three cents I think, now it is an investment.

When I think back I think we had a carefree life. We were cared for but not protected to death. Some kids are never out of sight of an adult, but I think they miss out.

MORE PRAISE FOR THE RED CROSS

Pathfinders, *Free Press Prairie Farmer*
June 14, 1944

Wilhemena Rosin (14)
Tomahawk, Alta.

Dear Pathfinders:

It's encouraging to see everyone doing their utmost to help the Red Cross and its magnificent life-saving work. It's up to us back here at home to help the Red Cross make it possible to supply our prisoners of war, soldiers and refugees with things they need. Let us all do what we can cheerfully and willingly.

Athlone school's Junior Red Cross club is still progressing nicely. We are knitting washcloths from warp and the girls are knitting sweaters. I was pleased when I read on this page that another school followed our idea of having a collection at each meeting.

I am sure everyone agrees that the Red Cross can't be beat. Here is a poem that I have written as a reminder.

This is surely an awful war,
There is always someone at your door,
Sure, you don't forget to pay your taxes,
But don't forget there is an Axis,
Whom we have got to help grind,
So get the subject on your mind,

Every penny that you save
Will help to dig the enemy's grave,
Keep buying stamps and war bonds, too,
Till your boys and friends are home with you.

BEING YOUNGEST HAD ITS ADVANTAGES

*Bill Wells, the youngest of a large family, recalls how his
older brothers and sisters kept the younger ones entertained.*

Here are a few memories of how I entertained myself before television. Actually, my father would not allow a radio in the house, so my memories pre-date radio in a sense. I am the youngest of a large family. My parents had fourteen children.

On Sunday evening my parents would sometimes go to church. My older brothers and sisters would gather all the chairs that were readily moveable. The chairs were laid on the floor, on their backs, in a "chain-like" fashion. We would pretend that we had a train. We would take turns being the engineer, the fireman, the conductor, the brakeman, or just a passenger. We could easily pass the evening making the sounds of the train, calling out the different stations, collecting tickets, etc. (Perhaps I should have said at the onset, we lived very close to the CNR marshalling yards so trains, boxcars, and steam engines and their noises were a very real part of our lives.)

On Saturday mornings, particularly in the winter, the youngest three would climb in bed with our older sister who would read us stories from *The Giant Book of Giant Stories*. The book was old, dog-eared, and yellowed with age. We knew all the stories from memory, long before we could read them for ourselves. I still can get a bit of a vicarious thrill as I recall the story of Molly Whoopee and the Bridge of One Hair. She always managed to escape from the giant by crossing the bridge, which he was too big to cross.

In the summertime my neighbourhood friends and I had little toy cars and trucks, some made out of cast iron, some of wood, some of tin. We would play for hours in the dirt of our backyard. We created roads, houses, sometimes whole villages.

Of course, we willingly supplied all the necessary sounds to make the scene live.

Often on Saturdays in the good weather we would "go for a hike," out into the country, about four miles from where we lived. My mother was sometimes too busy to make me a lunch, so she would give me 25 cents to go to the corner store and buy some cold meat and 2 buns to make my own sandwich. We would spend the day playing "cowboys and Indians" or "good guys and bad guys." We would walk there and back. At the end of the day we would return exhausted, ready for a hearty meal, and a good night's sleep.

Reading was also a passion with me. I would go to the local library and bring home four or five books each week. They became my "window on the world."

I was sixteen before I began to watch television.

GROWING UP IN THE OTTAWA AREA

Janet Emslie Reid, and her sisters Sandra and Dorothy, recall the games and activities of their childhood.

I am one of a family of six. I talked with sisters Sandra and Dorothy about our childhood and this is what we remembered. The time period was the mid-40s to mid-50s. The place was a semi-rural area just outside of Ottawa where we and our immediate neighbours lived on 10 acre farms—hobby farms they would be called today. We had cattle, chickens, sometimes a sheep or two, and sometimes a pig. Our neighbours had an apple orchard and raised mink and foxes. Beyond our little farms were proper Ottawa Valley mixed farms; in the other direction were houses on city-sized lots. There were 20 to 30 children in the immediate vicinity.

Most of the outdoor playing took place on the two small farms. Tag, with its many variations, was probably the most popular: Regular Hide and Seek, What time is it, Mr. Wolf? Red Light-Green Light, and Giant step-Baby step (we couldn't remember the name of this game).

A very popular variation of tag was called Run Sheep Run, played at dusk around the farm buildings and hay mow. There were two teams. All but the captain of team A hid. Then the A captain walked with the B captain and his team. The A captain would call out secret code warnings to his team when they were in danger of being found. (We couldn't remember if the team continually re-hid.) When it was deemed safe, A captain would call "Run Sheep Run" and his team would try to get to home before being tagged by team B members. This was a game for all ages and both sexes. Another popular game played by everyone was Rover Red Rover. It was quite rough but no one ever broke an arm.

Kite flying near Billings Bridge, Ottawa, 1930 (National Archives of Canada [PA 56384]).

Play in the winter included sledding, tobogganing, skating (never skiing), making igloos, snow forts, snowball fights, making angels, and fox and geese—another tag game but around a circle in the snow.

Marbles were played only in early spring, followed by ball games. Balls were bounced or thrown against a wall while the players clapped, threw the ball under a leg, or with their back to the wall (I vaguely remember quite elaborate variations). Baseball was a late spring and summer game played at school or on the flattest part of the pasture. Skipping was for girls and it also had many elaborate variations. Hopscotch was also a spring game. Other games included Go In and Out the Window, Here We Go Round the Mulberry Bush, Blind Man's Bluff and Statues ("It" flung people around and they had to freeze in the position in which they were flung—we can't remember what happened next.) Dodge ball was played at parties, but also at other times.

Girls played with paper dolls—either commercially made, cut out of the Eaton's Catalogue, or hand drawn. It was quite common to make clothes for all these dolls. We made up elaborate stories that sometimes lasted for days. Other times we traded dolls and clothes—usually the commercial ones.

Card games weren't too popular when I was young (Baptist father, Methodist mother), but Dorothy remembers Snap, Solitaire, and Old Maid. I remember dominoes, Chinese checkers, regular checkers, and crokinole.

And in our house, everyone read: fairy tales, L.M. Montgomery, I read Elsie Dinsmore, Albert Payson Terhune's collie stories, and all my Grandmother's books.

We went to Mission Band, Sunday School, and later to CGIT, but none of us were involved in Guides. Mother didn't drive and I don't think there was a group close by.

Writing down this list makes me wonder how we had time when chores came first, but we certainly had fun. My parents weren't handy so there were no homemade dolls, although we certainly played with dolls; there also weren't any games made by Dad. We used our imaginations to make up stories in the sandbox, while washing dishes or shelling peas. Sometimes we would put on a play or show of some sort and invited our parents and friends to see it.

I note that our games kept us physically active and were generally organized by ourselves. I feel sorry for children today whose activities are so often coloured by TV and computer games.

CUT OUTS AND OTHER GAMES

Janet Marshall grew up in Fredricton, New Brunswick. Whatever season of the year, Janet and her friends were busy.

I grew up in the 1930s and 40s and I had a great childhood. For the most part my childhood revolved around cut outs [paper dolls] — but these were cut outs that my talented friend drew, cut outs made from catalogues, or cut outs from books.

Some of the games we played included throwing a ball against a building and saying a rhyme or clapping our hands in different positions while catching the ball. We also played Red Rover in which two lines of children holding hands face each other. One side calls "Red Rover, Red Rover send Jane right over." Jane runs, trying to break through the opposite line. If she is successful, Jane goes back to her side, otherwise she becomes part of the opposition team. The side with all the people won. Other popular games included London Bridge, skipping with variations, clapping hands with variations, tag of different kinds, hide and seek, Simon Says, Red Light, croquet, marbles, and hand games such as scissors, paper, stone.

During the long winter months we used to ski, skate, toboggan, make snow houses or forts and, of course, play "I'm the King of the Castle and you're the dirty rascal" on high snow banks. Needless to say there were lots of snowball fights. In summer we went swimming, and biking, and played softball and "flies and grounders."

Like most little girls we loved dressing up in our mother's clothes. This was lots of fun, except my friend's mom was petite and wore high heels. Alas, I had big feet so I had to wear my mom's sensible shoes.

All the children in the neighbourhood had great fun putting on concerts in our garage — and we made money too!

Like all households we had lots of board games and as we grew older we played more difficult games including checkers and chess. My favorite time was visiting my grandparents and playing Chinese checkers and parcheesi with them and with my aunts. How could one manage without a pack of cards? One could play alone or with friends.

There was never a dull moment — perhaps that is why I can't understand it when my grandchildren complain, "I'm bored."

DAUPHIN FAIR

Pathfinders, *Free Press Prairie Farmer*
August 29, 1943

Olga Kudurudz
Shortdale, Man.

Dear Pathfinders:

Dauphin Fair was held July 10. The girls from our club were given tickets from Miss McConnell, and we also got a ride in a truck to the fair. Miss Herman, our teacher and leader, took us to the tent where we were registered.

There was a fashion parade for the girls — three girls from our club were in it. Then after the fashion parade there followed a parade of all the club boys and girls. In that parade there were 650 children. There were sewing clubs, swine clubs, grub [grain] clubs, garden clubs, and calf clubs. Following the parade Miss McConnell gave prizes for the best costumes worn.

My birthday is Nov. 15 and I am 13 years old. Have I a twin? I would like pen pals from Alberta and Saskatchewan. Letters with snaps will be answered first.

Pathfinders, *Free Press Prairie Farmer*
June 3, 1943

Mary Kett (14)
Marshall, Sask.

Dear Pathfinders:

I thought I should like to tell about the Girl Guides. I have belonged to the sisterhood of Guides for over a year now. I am patrol leader.

I think any girl that is interested should talk it over with other girls, and get in touch with those in authority and arrange to form a company. If a girl is by herself she may become a Lone Guide.

The Guides also heed the national outcry for assistance. The companies in our town have sent one shipment of clothes for the homeless victims in bomb-shattered Great Britain, and they are busily making more.

The training of a Girl Guide is an education in itself. She may learn many useful things. Proficiency badges are awarded any girl that excels in any occupation or hobby. Remember the future queen, Princess Elizabeth, is a Girl Guide.

CAMPING WITH THE GUIDES

Pathfinders, *Free Press Prairie Farmer*, n.d.

Nellie Mailie
Moose Jaw, Sask.

Dear Pathfinder.

Holidays are here again—holidays that mean swimming, camping, canoeing, and many other pleasant things.

I had the good fortune to attend Guide camp this year for a glorious week. One hundred and three girls attended the camp which was divided into four divisions called pink, purple, white and blue. Each tent was named so we called ours "Well-Come-In." Every morning at 7:15 the captain blew the whistle for rising and we all prepared for a dip in the cold water. We then prepared breakfast on stoves made by the camp girls. Later, after tidying up our tents, we had the color party gather where all in full Guide uniform gathered around the flag pole which centered the camp and sang "God Save the King." Then came inspection. The neatest tent in each division received a flag. For the rest of the day we engaged in treasure hunts, regatta and rest hour. In the evening we gathered and sang jolly songs and then "taps" to end our perfect day.

The last night of camp we had a masquerade where all types of costumes rigged up from uniforms, sheets, blankets and guide ties brought out many famous characters. I certainly enjoyed my first week at camp and hope to be able to go next year.

I would like correspondence—

BOY SCOUT WEEK

Pathfinders, *Free Press Prairie Farmer*
February 16, 1944

Dear Pathfinders—

Gather around Boy Scouts, Wolf Cubs, Girl Guides and Brownies; it's time I reminded you that the annual Boy Scout week in Canada begins Feb. 20 to Feb. 26. Tuesday, Feb 22, will be a special day for Boy Scouts and Girl Guides for it is the birthday of their founder, the late Baden-Powell who launched the Boy Scout Movement (as it is now called) in England in 1907-1908.

Work of the Boy Scout Movement is based on the idea of developing enthusiasm within the boy. The objective for the boy is good health, good character, and good citizenship.

Do you know, Pathfinders, that more than 120,000 members of Canada's navy, army and air force are former Boy Scouts? That's quite a record, isn't it? You might be interested too, in knowing what the Scouts have done on the home front. First, in practically every city, town or hamlet where a Boy Scout group exists, the Scouts and their young brothers the Wolf Cubs, have been active in the collection of salvage.

In Great Britain one of the problems is that of food production. Scouts over there have been operating Victory Gardens by the thousand, and hundreds of pounds of seed have been shipped to Britain by the Boy Scouts of Canada to make these Victory gardens possible. And of course, many hundreds of Canadian Boy Scouts have their own Victory Gardens.

— — —

The Wolf Cubs collect paper and magazines. They've made quilts which have gone to Britain for people who have been bombed from their homes. Other cubs have knitted dish towels, and still others have knitted hundreds of afghan squares and hospital shawls.

— — —

Boy Scouts have served as messengers, telegraph operators, first aid attendants (yes, Boy Scouts must learn first aid). They have also assisted in every Victory Loan campaign. Boys Scout have certainly done a grand job.

— — —

Every boy should be allowed the opportunity of belonging to the Boy Scouts. Not only are these boys trained for good citizenship but they will find it a lot of fun. If you are over eight years of age, and providing there is a Boy Scout group in you district, why not join during Boy Scout Week!

Here are the Scout Law and Scout Promise for those who may be interested. First the Scout promise: "On my honor I promise that I will do my best — To do my duty to God and King. To help other people at all times. To obey the Scout Law."

The Scout Law: 1. A Scout's honor is to be trusted. 2. A Scout is loyal. 3. A Scout's duty is to be useful and to help others. 4. A Scout is a friend to all and a brother to every Scout. 5. A Scout is courteous. 6. A Scout is a friend to animals. 7. A Scout obeys the orders of his parents, Patrol Leader or Scoutmaster without question. 8. A Scout smiles and whistles under all difficulties. 9. A Scout is thrifty. 10. A Scout is clean in thought, word and deed.

— Your Pathfinder-in-Chief.

A VERY BUSY CHILDHOOD

Whether playing a game, participating in other activities, or reading, Jean Wilson did so with great enthusiasm.

One of my earliest memories is of playing a game in Grade 2 at Susie Bawden Elementary School in Lethbridge where we formed two lines of kids holding hands. Then we'd say "Red Rover, Red Rover, we call xyz over" and that person from the other line would have to run across and try to break through our line. It could be a rough game sometimes, quite bruising. We must have played it a lot, though presumably we had other games as well. One was certainly Ante-I-Over, which involved throwing a ball over a roof and having someone on the other side of the house catch it. I don't think parents liked this game a lot, the danger always being that a ball would go through a window. By Grade 3 I know I played marbles, though not as voraciously as the boys, we girls being more inclined to play pick-up-sticks. All through elementary school there was a lot of playing on monkey bars, which seem in retrospect much harder and less interesting than what they seem to be now. And of course there were endless games of hopscotch, mainly the 10 step kind, not the version that was made up of layers of rectangles; and of skipping to various rhymes which I now don't remember. By Grade 4 or so I'm pretty sure I was heavily into softball, mainly because my Dad was a keen ball player and we started throwing balls to each other and playing softball when I was quite young. He probably taught me to throw, and certainly to throw like a boy, not a girl. I remember being quite scornful of girls who threw in that "silly" way many girls did/do. Nothing like the superiority of the very young!

At home I very early got hooked into doing puzzles, and from kindergarten on I was a keen reader, voraciously devouring anything I could find and even at 4 handing our copies of the Reader's Digest to visitors in our house because I obviously thought everyone should have something to read when they came to our house. Maybe it wasn't just Reader's Digest, though that certainly was one of the main magazines that my parents got, but they had others as well, and some books, too, usually Book-of-the Month Club ones.

Always there were games of make-believe, sometimes involving dolls but more often just pretend stuff without many props. I played a lot of cowboys and Indians without thinking much about the fact that that was mainly a boys' game. Growing up in southern Alberta and having a Mountie for a father I think made me particularly aware of the cowboy-Indian relationship. I saw Indians a lot, and I knew all about the Mounties first coming to Alberta to clear out the whisky traders and establish law and order and all that good stuff. I always got to be the one to do the reports about the Mounties, given my inside track to them, and some of my greatest childhood glory had to do with being occasionally driven to school by my Dad in a police car, even more occasionally when he had his red serge on. The more kids who saw me the better!

My parents were always keen card players, mainly of bridge, but they liked other games as well, and so my brother and I early on developed a taste for board games of all kinds, too. Snakes and ladders was a favourite, any number of versions of rummy and Snap, War, and solitaire were also popular. Chinese checkers and regular checkers were also popular in our house.

In Grade 3 I had a teacher who encouraged us to write stories, and from that year on I always had some kind of writing project. By the time I was in Grade 5 and in that horsey phase many girls, at least in Alberta, seem to go through, I was writing a novel, featuring a girl and a horse naturally. Before that I wrote 2-3 page stories, usually based on a picture from a magazine. One story I remember writing in Grade 3 class, not based on a picture, was the Easter story as I understood it. I got it more or less right, but did sound a note of scepticism at the end by concluding that Jesus said he'd come again, but he didn't say when. I remember being quite puzzled by that at the time, and obviously needed more certainty about his return that seemed to be given in the Bible.

THROUGH THE EYES OF A NEWCOMER

Tony Plomp shares his impressions of Canadian games.

I grew up as a child in Holland in the 1940s and came to Canada with my parents in 1951. For children of my generation and circumstances (sports activities were not emphasized in my family), soccer (voetbal) was the prime competitive sport. We played it in school during recess and lunch-breaks on our own with friends. The schools I attended during and after the Second World War had no gymnasiums or elaborate sports facilities and physical education as we know it in Canada was not part of my schooling. We made our own fun, riding around in "cars" built by our fathers, cruising on our bicycles to school and on self-motivated trips into the country-side and, during the winter, skating on the canals. There was a small lake near where we lived and my friends and I would sometimes rent a canoe or rowboat. Of course, in summer we swam, again in a tiny lake nearby, and, sometimes in fall and winter in public facilities. We also organized ourselves into "armies" and went about "conquering" various plots of undeveloped land north of our street. These battles did get bloody at times!

When I came to Canada I found myself as the proverbial "fish out of water." For one thing, physical education was part of the school curriculum and with it pressure from stern macho-type male teachers to perform. I always found myself inadequate before such types who seemed to devalue anyone who did not match their expectations.

For another, I found myself playing sports about which I knew nothing, such as baseball. Although I eventually learned some of the rules of the game and participated as necessary, it never enthused me. I found it a dull and lifeless kind of sport perhaps, in part, because I found it difficult to connect the bat to the ball! Where was "voetbal" (soccer)? People enthused about "football" which seemed to us a brutish kind of sport in which apparently the aim of the game was to injure your opponents and put them out of commission. Hockey was not a sport known to me, but I came to like watching it most because it seemed clear and clean and fast. It was like voetbal on ice!

Another sport that I had never encountered was lacrosse, which in my young immigrant days seemed more popular than today. I never played it but my future brother-in-law seemed heavily involved in it for a time. Basketball was also mostly foreign to me although I vaguely recall playing a game which I think was called "hoepbal." I remember that in Holland my father, who was manager of the Dutch office of Canadian Pacific Railways and Steamships, had "connections" which in 1950 included free tickets to a basketball game between a visiting Canadian and a Dutch team.

Everyone's experience is different. I think I was somewhat deprived of a healthy sports education and enthusiasm for sports and the like because of the very real limitations imposed by the years of war and their aftermath. In addition, my father, after a close brush with death in 1944, felt it necessary to devote most of his time to his family, his work, and his garden. He didn't have time to waste, not on sports anyway. Besides, his injuries prevented him from participating in any. (Although he took a daring two-mile bobsleigh ride in Switzerland in 1948 from one of its major mountains!) He frequently voiced his disapproval of people who would troop into the stadiums by their hundreds or thousands to watch soccer matches, and that on Sundays when these pagans should be in Church!!!

I find it interesting that today I still enjoy riding my bicycle and swimming most of all.

PAPER DOLL POEMS
by Polly King

Family Herald and Weekly Star
April 21, 1896

Dear little paper dolls, that grow
All in a beautiful, even row!
Their toes turn out in a way that's grand,
And they look so friendly, hand in hand.
I've boughten dolls put away on the shelf
For I love these best, that I make myself.

Then there come nice little paper boys
Who play with the girls, and break their toys.
They all have trousers down to their knees,
And they may shout just as loud as they please.
They never are bothered with dresses and curls,
And never are taken for little girls.

Of course there are cats in Paper Land,
    Or who would catch the rats?
They talk the language children talk,
And not the talk of cats.
    They say, instead of "purr," and "mew,"
"Good afternoon," and "How do you do?"

The paper folks don't always walk,
    But ride out every day;
Their horses go just like the wind,
    And do not care for hay —
They gallop in a long straight line,
    And really do look very fine.

Playing Is Playing Games

WE KNEW HOW TO HAVE FUN

Henry Barone, the son of Italian immigrants, grew up in Toronto during the 1920s and 1930s.

Sports and social activities dominated our free time. Many of the local service clubs such as the YMCA, Lions, Knights of Columbus, and other church organizations, sponsored youth clubs that organized hockey, basketball, volleyball, and baseball games and other community activities for youngsters.

Hockey was played on outdoor rinks, but while popular with players it had few fans. Only the hot-blooded would stand ankle deep in snow to cheer their favorite teams to victory. Players wore anything available in the way of warm clothing. Shin pads and knee pads were magazines stuffed under heavy woolen socks. Shoulder pads consisted of daily newspapers with holes cut large enough to put one's head through. Head gear and gloves were heavy woollen toques and thick gloves covered by leather mitts. Competing service clubs generally provided sweaters on loan. Six players and three alternates made up a hockey team, and it was not unusual for a shorthanded team to request an opposing coach to loan them a player in order to complete the game.

The cost for children to attend the Saturday matinee at the neighbourhood theatre was an astonishing six cents which usually included a bag of sticky, gooey candies or broken biscuits compliments of a nearby biscuit factory. (Adults were charged twenty-five cents.) To attend a children's Saturday matinee was an experience one would not quickly forget. It wasn't uncommon to see the screen being bombarded and splattered with over ripe fruit or sprayed with the contents of a Coke or Ginger Ale bottle (Pepsi Cola and 7-Up made their debut much later), not to mention that some mushy food may splatter your head and shoulders. Yes, even fish and chips made its grand appearance. Reason enough why the major theatres guardedly watched students as they entered. Adults were compelled to accompany children to the Saturday Matinee and that responsible adult had to be at least sixteen years old.

Cowboys and Indians was a Saturday ritual after the matinee show. The Indians' bows were made from discarded barrel staves from a nearby barrel company. Corset laces substituted for bow strings. The remainder of the corset would be used as body protection from flying arrows.

As a youngster there were many inventive games to play. Most street games required a minimum of equipment. To name a few: Kick the Can, Reliev'O, Sidewalk Tennis, Tap the Ice Box, Buck-Buck, Duck the Rock (I didn't, and this necessitated a trip to Children's Hospital for six stitches to close the wound on my head), Warble, One Strike and You're Out, Puck and Stick, Beat the Paddle, Chestnut Knockers, Spin the Hoop, Cross the Road Tag, plus a few DARE games. An orange box case with a couple of roller skates attached converted it into a scooter. Any kid who had a pair of roller skates made sure not to leave them on the porch overnight. Wheels from discarded carriages were nailed on the sides of apple boxes. Box car racing on Macadamized [paved] streets were noisy events. Teasing girls who were skipping rope was a must, as was disrupting their hopscotch games.

The sight of a bike-riding policemen scattered us in all directions. Bikes were licensed at fifty cents a year. Horse-drawn fire reels were redundant, and the majority of Fire Stations had motorized Fire Engines. The clank, clank, clanking of the fire engines out on call attracted all youngsters within hearing distance.

The Depression years changed our lifestyle. Churches converted their basements and small gathering rooms into playschools during the day and recreational gatherings in the evenings. One day a week was set aside for youth social activities and a night or two for basketball and volleyball. Saturday nights we gathered at one of the homes for "come-as-you-are" or pajama parties—all strictly monitored by parents. A banana party was a big attraction at our home. The menu consisted of banana fritters, banana sandwiches, banana cookies, banana cakes, banana pies, banana fries, and finally thin slices of the banana stock dipped in a batter and pan fried. It was so successful it sparked a series of fruit parties. Fortunately, a few of our friends' families operated fruit stores.

The Depression proved a boon to children. The Maple Leafs, of the international baseball league, introduced the "Knot-Hole" club. All members of the Girls and Boys Clubs were issued membership cards giving them free admission to the Saturday baseball games. Babe Ruth and other stars of that era mingled with the youngsters for a short while after the game. The CNE [Canadian National Exhibition] and the Royal Winter Fair had children's days which included free streetcar rides to the grounds and the horse palace. During the hot weather months the Toronto Transportation Commission offered free rides to the beaches between the hours of 10 A.M. and 4 P.M. All playgrounds were supervised and equipment supplied. The Youth Clubs and playgrounds competed in track and field as well as ball games.

An empty lot at Church and Carlton Streets was our playing field until Con Smythe built his empire there. The Maple Leaf Gardens blossomed quickly. With it came the birth of "HOCKEY NIGHT IN CANADA," and Foster Hewitt was its Master's voice.

LEFTY WILSON AND THE NAKED LADY

Reprinted with permission from Hal C. Sisson and Dwayne W. Rowe,
Coots, Codgers and Curmudgeons: Things Were More Like They Used To
Be Then Than They Are Now (Victoria: Orca Books, 1994).

A good marble player requires a good eye, a good finger, a
good shooter, a competitive spirit, and a bit of luck. Hal C.
Sisson was, and still is, an ardent marble player.

Lefty

Grade eight is about the limit of your marble playing days. You played in spring. Almost before the first robin started hopping on the lawn, out came the marbles. Then, a few weeks later, almost as suddenly as they had appeared, the marbles were gone. Most everyone played, and most everyone gambled their marbles, but by grade eight, Lefty Wilson and I were the two players most feared on the school playground. We were never friends per se, always seeming to travel in the different little groups that keep forming and reforming in public school. Except at marble time — then we were friendly rivals who met often.

I spoke of a lawn, of which we had very little at Christopher. What we did have was a level gravel pit with some very hardy weeds around the edges, surrounded by a caragana hedge and a line of bedraggled trees on the boulevard. On this surface the serious marble players would kick out all the rocks and stones, then scuff the dirt surface as smooth, flat and hard as possible, and draw a ring. Serious poker players won't play outlandish card games with wild cards, like Midnight Baseball or Piss in the Ocean, only playing Draw or Stud. So we too no longer played what we considered dumb games like Chasies, Holy Bang, Funsies or Bung-hole. We would on occasion play Poison Ring, Black Snake or Killer, which were games for the best shooters. The most popular was the real national rules game called Ringer. You had to shoot with ease and deadly accuracy to do well in that game. Otherwise you lost all your marbles.

Ringer was played in a ten-foot-diameter circle with each player placing an equal number of marbles in the centre of the ring in the form of a cross. Knock a marble out and it was yours.

You set your own rules when you played for keeps, and usually you had to knuckle a certain number out while shooting from the edge of the ring, before you could dribble in amongst the remaining dibs. That position could be dangerous because if another player knocked out your shooter you were out of the game. Well, you probably all know the rules anyway.

Boys playing marbles in a Vancouver schoolyard, 1950 (ArtRay Collection, Vancouver Public Library, Special Collections [81192]).

The players inspected the agates that were being wagered to be sure that they were playing for approximately equal value. Nobody wanted to put up a spotless lemon corkscrew against a chipped swirl. The kids had an unwritten code of marble values.

The Marbles

The names probably change with the years. Marbles aren't played as much as they used to be, before TV and all the modern distractions. But often what kids called marbles made more sense than the names the makers gave them. Names such as snakes and 7 Up's, bumble-bees, the cub scout, the black widow or wasp. There were blue moon and foggies, and a gassie that looked like a puddle of water with gasoline in it.

The Gamble

Good marbles is much like shooting good pool. How you hit the object dictates where your shooter is going to come to rest. Just as in snooker, "English" can be obtained; in marbles the thumbs act in the same manner as the cue tip—under the marble for backspin, toward the top for topspin. Strategy calls for not leaving your shooter in the ring if you fail to knock out one of the dibs. If you stun the target marble, it goes out and your shooter stays very near the point of impact, ready to take your next shot at another nearby marble. The closer you stay to the marbles left in the ring, the more you clean up. But at times you want to strike the object marble on the side in order to get your shooter to carom to another part of the ring. But sometimes and for some reason, the dib does not quite depart the ring, and worse still, your shooter stays in the ring also, sometimes uncomfortably close to the edge. It is now no longer your shot as you haven't made a dib, you can't run for cover by purposely shooting out, and you are at the mercy of your opponent. Ten feet is a long distance to accurately knuckle a small marble, but good players are extremely accurate—and when you cut this distance down to one or two feet, someone is likely to go down the tubes.

On my first shot of the last game, I hit two mibs, my shooter and one marble exiting the ring, but leaving a snooger, which is a "commie rat" target marble near the rim of the ring. It was a good set-up for my next shot but I made a "mistook"—I called "slips." But the Naked Lady had travelled far more than ten inches and therefore had to be considered a shot. I was now left vulnerable in the ring; Lefty yelled "fan, everies" and circled the playing ring, seeking his best playing position. He knuckled down, preparing to ride the snooger by hitting it a glancing blow, knocking it from the ring, while bouncing his shooter into the mass of easy target marbles and my shooter in the centre. I was as good as dead in the dirt in this game.

Marbles do many different things. The snooger didn't have to move very far to go out of the ring; so Lefty aimed too soft a shot at the right side of the snooger—a near miss and his shooter spun madly in some loose dirt, slowing its progress until it came to rest within easy range of the Naked Lady.

And that's what happened to Lefty. I "killed" him and won the Shoot Out. It was the last game of marbles I ever played. The marble season was over for all time.

A FINE COASTING TRAY

Maple Leaf Club, *Family Herald and Weekly Star*
March 18, 1914

MARIPOSA LILY
Rock Creek, B.C.

Dear Maple Leaves:

My sister and I have a nice coasting path, and we have fun on it in the afternoons after our lessons are done. Our mother gives us lessons every day. We have one ordinary coasting sled, two home-made barrel stave sleds, and best of all, an old iron tea tray. And oh, Leaves, it is such fun going down on the tray. You can make it spin round and round if you like, but it will go straight, too. It seems to go faster if you go down backwards; it's because you can't see in front, I expect.

We also have two pairs of skis. They go better near Spring when there is a crust on the snow.

MADE A PAIR OF SKIS

Maple Leaf Club, *Family Herald and Weekly Star*
March 14, 1917

Clarence Orser
CYCLIST
Kingston, R.R. #4, Ont.

Dear Maple Leaves:

Here comes another Leaf to join the Great Tree. I am fourteen years old, and live on a farm seven miles north of Kingston.

I have a bicycle and in summer I get a great deal of pleasure out of it. On cool summer nights I often ride to Kingston and take in the show, at other times a crowd of boys will gather together at Elginburg (our home village) and go swimming in Collin's Creek. In the spring we spear fish in the same creek. We have a rink near our house and every winter we have lots of fun skating on it.

I made a pair of skis. The first time I tried them I started down a steep hill behind the house; when I was about halfway down they turned around on me and this threw me on my back. Then I tried putting them together and so made a sort of toboggan. This time I met with little success, for they seemed to want to turn around in spite of me. At last I got tired of that kind of skiing and tried it standing up. This time I went down the hill all right; after that I could manage them a little better.

I have thought a lot about getting a rifle. I like hunting rabbits or any kind of animals. About five years ago my two brothers and a neighbor's boy went hunting, but when they saw the first bear track they must have got a little skittish for they came home in about two weeks.

I would like to correspond with any boys or girls, especially Sumac Bob. I promise to answer all letters.

TENNIS AND GOLF

Maple Leaf Club, *Family Herald and Weekly Star*
August 22, 1917

ANEMONE

Dear Ex-Leaves:

I live in a large town were there are very many attractions for young people but lately I find many of these dull and insipid. Among the many interesting things are a great variety of sports of which I was at first a great lover. These were hockey, baseball, basket ball, tennis and golf. Of the last two I never get tired.

This town does quite a bit for the boys at the front, having many clubs, etc., in looking after their welfare. Several of these I belong to, and indeed am quite fond of the work.

I find it interesting if I take a magazine to a hospital and read to the patients. They really appreciate any little favors. If anyone should wish to correspond with me I would be delighted as I think it must be great fun to hear about all the other interesting towns and doings of this little old world.

THE GAMES KIDS (USED TO) PLAY

Used with permission from Ina Trudgeon, *A Backward Glance* (unpublished manuscript).

Ina Trudgeon grew up in the Fairview district of Vancouver during the 1920s.

Street games were common in the twenties and thirties. We just moved to the ditch when we heard the familiar "ah-oo-gah" of the occasional car.

Eighth Avenue was a macadamized road with deep ditches and high banks. The boys on the street made a glorious swing from the telephone pole. There were L shaped spikes driven all the way up the pole, meant for repairmen to climb the pole to repair the wires. Some brave lad climbed by the spikes to near the top where he attached a thick rope reaching the ground. A loop for sitting was made at the end of the rope. With feet pressed against the bank, one could give a mighty "push-off," swing far out from the bank and around the pole in a half circle, landing with a thump on one's feet on the other side of the pole. What a thrill! We never thought of the dangers; a wrongly directed push could have sent one crashing into the pole, or the rope could have broken. However, I don't remember any mishap. Anyway, kids always think they are immortal.

Stilts were all the rage at the time. There were matched tin cans with thin ropes knotted through holes punched in each side with a big nail. These ropes were held in the hands in order to keep your feet in contact with the top of the cans as you walked along with your feet about five inches off the ground. A more adventuresome kind of stilt was made of 2 by 4s which gave one added height of about three feet. The high ones had to be mounted from a fence and then you really felt like a giant among the Pygmies. Buzz, our uncle, made me a pair from some scrap lumber, since I was the tomboy of the family. I got so adept on these things that I could almost run with them.

The boys made soapbox cars, which we called "bugs," from old wooden apple boxes attached to roller-skate wheels and tin cans nailed to the front as head lights. The only means of propulsion was being pushed or going down hill. Scooters were a different style with the apple box mounted upright on a board to which roller-skate wheels were attached. The propelling was done with one foot while standing on the board with the other. Most boys, also, had a commercially made "little red wagon," often used for getting groceries or delivering papers.

Soapbox derby (Wrathall Collection, Prince Rupert City and Regional Archives and Museum of Northern B.C.).

Skip was played both at school and on the sidewalk in front of our house. A long rope was held by two "turners" and as soon as someone missed a skip, she had to take the rope. We got really skillful at this and when single skipping bored us, we switched to "double Dutch." This entailed doubling the rope and then, with a rope in each hand, the "turners" alternated turning each rope. The skipper had to be doubly quick, alternating each foot to clear each rope as it hit the sidewalk.

"Salt, vinegar, mustard, pepper!" On the word "pepper," the "turners" would turn the rope as fast as they could while the skipper tried to keep up—but not for long.

There were endless rhymes for skip. Every time you skipped this rhyme you were dealt a different husband according to where you missed the rope.

Tinker, Tailor, soldier, sailor,
Doctor, lawyer, Indian Chief,
Rich man, Poor man,
Begger-man, thief.

I know that I had no idea what a tinker was and there was always a laugh at your expense if you missed the rope on begger-man or thief. The rhyme went on to predict the whole wedding as to gown, vehicle, and time.

Silk, satin, cotton, rags.
Coach, carriage, wheelbarrow, dumpcart.
This year, next year, sometime, never.

We had a few slightly rude rhymes which we didn't repeat before Mother:

I see London, I see France,
I see Mary's (or whomever's) dirty pants.

And anyone hit with bird-droppings would console himself singing,

Darned old sea gull,
It's a good job cows can't fly.

There were several old sayings kids had, some of which would be a response to a situation such as being teased by name-calling:

Sticks and stones may break my bones,
But names will never hurt me.

My face I don't mind it. I'm behind it.

It's the folks out in front get the jar.

or

Go home and tell your mother she wants you.

If you wanted to feel a little superior you would climb a fence, a tree top, or a stump in a vacant lot (there were lots of vacant lots in Vancouver then, filled with native shrubs such as pussy willow, huckleberry, salmonberry, and blackberry) and proclaim:

I'm the king (never the queen) of the castle
And you're the dirty rascal.

My! What mild verbal clashes, compared with what even small children use today.

There were some boys' games at which girls were mostly bystanders, such as Knife, Peggy, and Marbles. Knife was played with a jack knife, the tip of the blade was poised on each finger in turn and flung off to stab into the ground as far away as possible. Peggy necessitated digging a hole across which was placed a short section of an old broomstick. A longer piece of broomstick was used to fling the first stick into the air in order to whack it as high and as far as you could. This game was discouraged at school because of all the holes that were made in the school grounds. Marbles was a great favourite with most boys, but some were so skilled at shooting the other players' marbles out of the circle that they cornered the market and amassed a great stockpile.

Girls occupied their rainy winter days with a number of activities. Embroidering tea cloths and dresser scarves was popular. This required the transfer of a pattern with a hot iron onto a cloth and mastering a variety of stitches using brightly coloured embroidery thread. These included French knots and the lazy daisy stitch. We also did spool knitting. This required an empty cotton spool with four headless phonograph needles pounded into the top of the spool on which to wind the yarn to make a long braided cord. This could be used to make rugs for a doll house, a table mat, or, if especially ambitious, perhaps a bedside rug.

There was also the winter fun in the snow. Our favourite hill was on Ash Street between Broadway and Sixth Ave. The only light was one lamp at each intersection, although the snow brightened the night considerably. The hill was not officially blocked off, but we posted a guard at each intersection with a "bug" consisting of a tin can with a wire handle affixed and a large hole cut in the side so the light of a candle could shine out. If a car was approaching an intersection, the "bug" was waved frantically to warn the sledder coming down the hill to head for a snowbank in the ditch.

A GAME OF WAR

Maple Leaf Club, *Family Herald and Weekly Star*
August 15, 1915

Laura Whitelaw
BINGO
Guelph, Ontario
(Your game of "war" sounds most realistic, and it must have been very exciting. — Editor.)

Dear Maple Leaves:

I am going to tell you about a game we played at school. "War" it is called. All the boys dressed as soldiers, they had strips of cloth from their right shoulder to their left side, and they had pieces of cloth wound around their legs. The general and most of his men wore tissue paper caps, and had pieces of cloth with brass buttons on their shoulders. (Last of all, they had swords made of wood.)

We girls were dressed as Red Cross nurses. We wore pieces of white cloth with red crosses on our left arms and white caps on our heads. We divided into two equal sides; the school was our hospital.

The war was held in the woodshed where some wood was piled up and the boys made trenches of it. We got some snow for bullets and put it in the trenches. The gun was fired and the war began. For a while the bullets flew as fast as hail and hit many soldiers, and many men lay dead on the field. They seemed to come into the hospital very fast, and we were kept busy bandaging their wounds. But, at last, the British crept closer and closer to the German trenches and fired a volley which knocked down their trenches and killed many of their men. There they were, fighting face to face, it was a terrible scene. But the British would not yield, and the Germans found it useless to try to capture the British trenches, so the flag was put up. Don't you think King George would have been pleased had he seen them fighting so bravely?

A SKATING PARTY

Pathfinders, *Free Press Prairie Farmer*
January 6, 1924

Ruth Pinder (13)
Springside, Sask.

Dear Pathfinders,

I am going to tell you of some the pleasure we have skating. Some of the young people and myself go down to the river about a quarter of a mile from our place to skate. When it gets cold the boys make a big fire, and then we get warm and we go skating again. This is how we spend our winter evenings.

I have a mile to go to school, but we are having our holidays now; we are going to have no school for a month or two.

I have two sisters and two brothers. I must close now and would like to have someone of my own age write to me.

MAKING A RINK

Pathfinder Page, *Free Press Prairie Farmer*
January 1, 1919

Theodore Holden (9)
Boissevain, Man.

Dear Pathfinders:

This is my third letter to your club. I have been reading them for a long time. I found them very interesting. I am going to tell about our neighbour's curling rink. The boys chose a good spot for it. There were three ponies working. All the rest had sleighs with boxes on them, and were hauling snow for the sides and ends. We flooded it about four times a day for about a week. Then we got two tanks of water. We have a little shanty with a stove in it, and it is lovely and warm when we have the fire going. There are benches in there. I would like to correspond with any boy my own age.

WE ORGANIZED OURSELVES

Freda Mallory grew up in Terrace, British Columbia.

The games we played required little or no equipment, and what equipment was needed was generally something that was lying around. We didn't need parent groups to organize the games or provide equipment—and we never thought of, or mentioned, being "bored." Our parents had good remedies for boredom, like weeding the garden or filling the woodbox or whatever.

Running Games

Many of our games required a lot of physical activity. Tag in its varied forms was always popular. This meant one person "It" tried to catch another person who would them become "It."

Fox and Hare: (Fox and Goose in other areas) was a popular variation of tag. Traditionally, Fox and Hare was always played after the first snowfall and continued through the winter. A large circle was tramped down, paths are tramped across the diameter of the circle, thereby cutting the circle into six, eight or more segments. The Fox was in the middle. The other players (Hare) were on the outer ring. The venture is for the Hares to go as far as they can on the spokes without being caught by the Fox. They must stay on the outer ring or the spokes of the circle. The one who is caught then becomes "Fox."

Games such as Run Sheep Run, Red Rover, Pom Pom Pull-away, Prisoner's Base, and Auntie-I-Over were running games that involved two opposing teams. The purpose was to secure more players for your side. When these games were played enthusiastically they could become quite rough. Leap Frog and Follow the Leader were also active running games.

Another group of games including What Time is it, Mr. Wolf? Go, Go, Stop! Mother May I? required players to move from a starting line to a finish line without being caught by "It." Other active but less strenuous games included Blind Man's Buff and Simon Says.

Musical Games

Musical games were usually played by small children and young girls. Boys over age eight tended to view singing games as "sissy stuff." These games could be played either indoors or outdoors, depending on the weather and the time of the year. We enjoyed London Bridge, I Wrote a Letter to My Love, The Farmer's in the Dell, Here We Go Looby Loo, The Grand Old Duke of York, Ring Around a Rosie, and Here We Go Round the Mulberry Bush.

Other Outdoor Games

Scrub was the neighbourhood version of baseball. It required few players and minimal equipment. If we were lucky, someone would have a ball and a real bat, but generally we played with an old tennis ball or whatever ball was around and any stick or piece of wood that could hit the ball. When the batter was "out" he went into the field and the next player was at bat.

When Marbles and Jacks came out we knew it was spring. Both boys and girls played marbles, but Jacks tended to be a girls' game. Skipping, whether individually, Double Dutch or China Skip was a girls' game as girls were more adept skippers than boys.

There were many versions of Hopscotch ranging from fairly simple to quite difficult hopscotch diagrams We drew our hopscotch diagrams on the ground with sticks, and our "counters" or "markers" were usually small pieces of wood or stones or whatever was lying around. We played a number of ball bouncing games. These were usually done to a rhyme that set a specific order for bouncing the ball on the ground, off parts of the body, or off a wall.

Of course we made Snow Angels in an area of freshly fallen snow. We played "good guys-bad guys" games including Cowboys and Indians or Cops and Robbers. With a few bits and pieces, and a little imagination, we played house, store and school.

Indoor Games

We usually received board games as Christmas or birthday gifts. I still have my checker board set that I received about seventy years ago. Other games included Dominoes, Tiddly Winks, Snakes and Ladders, Pick-Up-Sticks, and Crokinole. And we played card games such as Rummy, Old Maid, Go Fish, Hearts , Snap, and Solitaire. I Spy was another favorite. One player says "I spy with my little eye something that begins with 'C' or is 'red.'" The others try to guess what it is. The successful person then does the "spying."

Party games included Pin the Tail on the Donkey, or Pin the Nose on the Clown, or Pin the Mouth on the Jack-O-Lantern, depending on the season of the year. We also played Hide the Thimble, Button, Button, Who's Got the Button? and I Packed My Bag.

My sister and I spent a lot of time reading. Books were always among our Christmas gifts.

Once in a while we played what we called Duck on a Rock. A small rock (duck) was set on top of a large rock. We then stood around and threw stones at the duck in an effort to knock the duck off the rock. It was quite dangerous as we could have hit other children with our stones, and our teachers and parents forbid us playing it.

As I look back I realize what a busy, happy childhood I had.

EVERY SEASON HAD ITS ACTIVITIES

Margaret Walker recalls the games and activities of her late 1930s Saskatoon childhood.

School and Recess Games

These included skipping, soft ball, marbles, volley ball, and roller skating (metal wheels on the sidewalk).

We bounced a hard Indian rubber ball off the windowless side of the school while following a set routine of claps before catching the ball: plainsies, clapsies, roly poly, etc. The ball was also bounced on the sidewalk while the bouncer went through a certain series of routines. We often engaged in Yo-yo and Bolo bat competitions and demonstrations.

Winter Games

Fox and Geese (always after the first snow fall), broom ball on ice, snow angels, skating, and sliding down snow banks on cardboard were the usual games.

Street Games

After supper all the kids on the block played games such as Hide and Seek, Tag, Arrows, or Hoist Your Sails.

Arrows: In this game Team One hides, drawing arrows along the way, sometimes leaving mis-cues. Team Two follows, and as soon the first team is sighted they all dash for home.

Hoist your Sails (Oyster Sails or Oyster Shells): Team One hides, a member comes back to "home" and draws a map of where team one went. Team two follows the route (shortcuts sometimes), after sighting Team One they dash back to "home."

Other Street Games: Red Light, Simon Says, and Red Rover were played on the street because there were so few cars. Girls played hopscotch and jacks on the sidewalk in front of their houses. In the summer we would set up a lemonade stand and sell glasses of (watery) lemonade for 2 cents. The mailman would always buy. We prepared and presented neighbourhood concerts in someone's garage. The charge would be 5 cents per person. Our parents usually attended.

Dolly Dingle (cut-outs) were great favourites. Old catalogues provided extensive wardrobes for the dolls and furniture for the houses we made out of boxes. We had proper books of cutouts, but they really weren't as much fun as the catalogue variety. Putting the dolls in the pram and taking them out for a walk was always popular. I always wanted an "Eaton's Beauty" but I guess our Santa couldn't afford it.

One of my most cherished possessions was a lovely big singing top. Board games were very popular: Snakes and Ladders, Parcheesi, Crokinole (if your finger could take it), Checkers, Pick-up-Sticks, Chinese Checkers, and card games. We spent hours playing house, school, church, and having tea parties. Reading was a great passion. So was listening to the radio, and the whole family did this together.

For us, highlights would be the school concerts, school assemblies (top floor of the school), Sunday School picnics, and Christmas concerts. Halloween would be a great adventure when we'd try to remember where we got the good home-made fudge the year before—far cry from where children can go today and what they are allowed to eat! We usually had a song or a poem that was required before the treat was dropped into the pillowcase.

When we went to Vanscoy to visit we join the local children on their trek to the station to meet the passenger train. It was an important event in their day.

This has been great fun recalling the carefree, innocent days of childhood—putting on skates and skating down the block to the outdoor rink at Caswell School lit by the corner street light. We would come home half-frozen, but it was great fun.

A SKATING PARTY

Pathfinders, *Free Press Prairie Farmer*
January 16, 1924

Gwyneth Davies (13)
Heart Lake, Alta.

Dear Pathfinders,

We live by a small lake called Heart lake, so I can have many a pleasant skate. We had a skating party here this fall. There were 19 people present. We skated until 11, then we had lunch and played games till 4. I have no brothers or sisters, I am 13 and in grade eight. I ride to school on a pony; his name is Tipperary. I can crochet, knit and embroider. I also like to read. I would like to hear from any girls my own age. Wishing the members a prosperous new year.

GAMES OF WAR

Fred Greaves recalls his wartime childhood in Vancouver.

I entered Grade 1 at Vancouver's Cecil Rhodes School in 1939, right at the start of World War II. It was a fear-filled time. As a little boy I became acquainted with constant air-raid drills, the buying of 25 cent war stamps, rationing, the ARP (Air Raid Precaution) with constant blackouts and the fearful notion that the walls had ears. The war spilled over into our games. We built cities out of cardboard boxes and had air raids on them. We made wooden guns of the type used in the war. We knew all the types of planes used by both sides because we collected them from the backs of Player's cigarette packages. The climate of the times seemed to determine the nature of the games we played. The distrust and violence engendered by war was reflected in the competitive (often violent) ways in which the games were played. In our war games we use slingshots and BB guns and at times people got really hurt.

Racism was very much alive. Race-based stories abounded. I remember a Chinese gentleman wanted to buy my dog. My friends said he wanted to use it for meat, and I believed them. The Jewish boys were always targeted. We would make fun of them, often not knowing why. One day in about grade 3 or 4 all the Japanese boys and girls in my class were no longer there. We were told they had gone back to Japan—which was a blatant lie.

Child in toy airplane, 1920 (Frank Leonard Collection, Vancouver Public Library, Special Collections [12626]).

The by-products of war were everywhere and many of our games took on this flavor. The Saturday afternoon movies always contained the newsreels and some of the footage was terrible in its brutality. The radio programs I listened to each afternoon were all violent, i.e., Terry and the Pirates (the pirates were the Japanese), Superman fighting global conquest, The Green Hornet, The Shadow, and so on. It is interesting that sex played very little part in our world and drugs played no part in either elementary or secondary grades.

But to repeat, our games and interpersonal relationships were quite violent. Cigarette smoking was very common. Hobbies usually centred on collecting and trading, i.e., marbles, pictures of airplanes and warships from the back of Player's cigarette packages, and building models again of war ships and planes. During the high school years the in thing was to join the cadets.

Games Played by Elementary School Boys (1939-49)

Cut the Pie: You played against an opponent. The circle was cut in half. You tossed a coin for who would go first. Player A would throw down his knife and if it stuck blade first in player B's semicircle, a radius was drawn through the knife. Player A continued until his knife did not stick in the ground. Then player B would continue. You always threw from whatever sector you had left. You could use one foot. The game ended when your opponent's sector was so small he could no longer stand in it.

Pom-Pom Polaway [Pullaway]: This game consisted of 2 teams. One stationed at one end of the field and one in the middle. The aim was for the team at the end of the field to run the gauntlet to the other end of the field without being brought down by the kids in the centre. If you were caught and wrestled to the ground you joined the team in the centre. The winner was the last boy to run the gauntlet. (It reminded one of games played by the Mongol warriors.) The kids in the middle were allowed to pile on. A less violent form of the game required only a tag on the back of the people running. Many students were hurt in this game.

Ships and Sailors: Again we used two teams. One team bent over—head between the fellow's legs in front of you with the lead man's shoulder against a tree trunk. The other team would run and jump and straddle on the backs of the boys bent over. The score was kept of the fewest number of boys it took to collapse the other side. It goes without saying that the heaviest boys were always chosen first for either team. This also was a very dangerous game.

Marbles: It seemed like every boy played marbles. Most collections contained catseyes (glass), dough-babies (clay), and steelies (ball bearings of various sizes). The large glass marbles were called cobs.

(a) Square Pot: You drew a square pot on the ground. You placed one of your marbles in the pot and your opponent did the same. You both went back to the line and tossed your alley to the pot. The closest to the pot went first and the aim was to knock your opponent's alley out of the pot. If you did you kept it.

(b) Round Pot: You played against one or more opponents. You and your enemies put a specified number of marbles in the pot. You drew sticks to see who would go first, second, etc. You shot from the circumference and the idea was to knock your opponent's marbles out of the pot. If you did you kept his marbles. If you missed your opponents' marbles you lost your turn—you tried to put the smallest marble you could into the pot (usually steelies) and shot with a cob.

(c) Stink Pot: You played against one or more opponent. You started from a line and tried to get your marble into a series of holes, until you reached the finish line. You could only take one shot at a time. You alternated your shots. The first boy finished kept the other boys' marbles.

Chestnuts: Some kids called the game "Conkers," but we never did. You drilled a hole in the chestnut and ran a shoelace through with a knot at the end. The idea was to try to hit and break your opponent's chestnut. We tried everything we could to harden and dry up our chestnuts to make them harder to break.

Yo-Yos: This was a seasonal game. All of a sudden yo-yos would show up all over the school yard. There were various grades of yo-yos. The 25 cent ones were 2 colours with a coloured stripe through the centre. The 50 cent ones were silver and the 75 cent ones were gold. This was really a game of skill. Some of the tricks included: around the world, over the falls, rock the cradle, walk the dog, in the pocket, three-leaf clover, and so on. (Most of these I can still do.) The real skill came in using a yo-yo in each hand. The yo-yos had a Cherrio label on them and often a Cherrio champ would come to the school and demonstrate tricks and hold competitions. You might win new strings, a new yo-yo, or even a pass to the movies.

Bolo Bats: These were also seasonal. These were not as popular as yo-yos. The bats were of 2 kinds. One was a thin 3 ply bat and this cost 25 cents, and the other a thicker 5 ply bat that cost 35 cents. The idea was to keep hitting the ball which was attached to a long rubber band as many times as you could in succession. One trick was to turn your bat over and keep things going. The real skill, again, came in one bat in each hand at the same time.

Senior Elementary and Junior High Years (grades 7, 8, 9)

Soapbox Races: We made our own soapboxes—there were few restrictions. Steep hills would be roped off and we would race on these hills. Some outside organization—probably from some companies involved in automobile manufacture or the oil companies—seemed to be involved in sponsoring the races. (I believe some winners had a chance to compete in Akron, Ohio. We never got that far.)

Scrub Baseball, Roller-Hockey, and Soccer Games: There were few formally organized sports leagues so we made our own. The teams were usually picked from certain geographical areas in the city, Main Street, Oak Street, Kerrisdale, and so on. These leagues seemed to maintain themselves and competition was intense. The amazing thing about this was the efficient communication system we had. We always seemed to know when and where the games would be played.

Ice-Hockey: For most of us, this was restricted to limited times on Beaver Lake, Lost Lagoon, or some local pond. Here again, the communication network was truly amazing.

SCOTCH GAMES AT BANFF

Pathfinders, *Free Press Prairie Farmer*
January 8, 1930

Walter Kenyon (14)
Mara, B.C.

Dear Pathfinders,

I went for a holiday to Banff during the summer and I will tell you about the Scotch sports they had there.

On Friday afternoon there was dancing and the piping of the Lament. On Saturday there was more piping; this time of songs and marches. There was also dancing. I liked the sword dance best. A sword and its scabbard were crossed and they danced in the angles it formed. If they touched either the sword or the scabbard they were disqualified. Men were throwing around metal discs at pieces of paper stuck in the ground. On Sunday there was a sermon by Ralph Connor in the morning. That afternoon there was an open-air concert of singing, piping, and marching. On Monday there were all kinds of athletic sports, including races—both dashes and long distance—pole vaulting, high jump, broad jump, javelin throw, and piping and dancing.

I would like to hear from members in the north or anywhere.

PLAYING MARBLES THE ST. JOHN'S WAY

Helen Porter, *Below the Bridge: Memories of the South Side of St. John's* (St. John's: Breakwater Press, 1979). Published with the permission of Breakwater Press. Copyright the author.

Helen Porter recalls playing marbles South Side style.

Somebody once defined heaven as "one eternal summer day." I suppose the summers I spent on the South Side were no different from Newfoundland summers generally—short, with plenty of rain and cool weather, and the occasional hot sunny day. But in my memory that's not the way they were at all. Summer was very long, something like a rainbow that stretched from school closing in June to that distant day in September when it would open again. And the pot of gold wasn't at the end of it but had been emptied out and distributed throughout the seventy or eighty days of glorious freedom. I know there must have been summer days when we were bored silly, when we quarrelled and cried and sulked. But like the pains of childbirth, those days are quickly forgotten, at least by the conscious mind. The gold shines brightly, as gold should, and as the years pass it becomes even more lustrous.

We prepared for summer long before school closed. On the first sunny day in March the marbles came out and though the wind blew bitterly and our hands were numb and blue with cold, gloves were discarded and often lost. If there was any strength at all in the sun's rays, coats and caps were tossed in a pile on a fence or rail. "The mot is alive," someone would shout even as somebody else was shouting "The mot is dead." I tried in vain to discover the origin of the word "mot," and I don't even know if I'm spelling it correctly. It is, of course, the small round hole, dug first with the heel and then smoothed out with the fingers, toward which the small clay marbles are thrown or rolled, and its life or death status makes a great deal of difference to the game, for if the mot is dead the marbles that roll into it are worthless for points, while if it lives it can add greatly to the score. Later on the drab little clay marbles were replaced by dazzling glass alleys, which were still being used the last time I checked out a game. We also liked to get hold of little shiny metal ball bearings. We called them ballbearions, and like the more exotic glass ones, they were always in great demand. If you managed to win some at a mot game or at "Chip, chip, how many" your partner would often decide that you really hadn't been playing for keeps.

CHILDHOOD GAMES IN THE YUKON
IN THE 1930S

Hugh was eight and Jim was four when the McCullum family left Dawson City for the "outside."

Hugh recalls: As a child in the Yukon in the 1930s it seems we were much the same as other kids of that period. There wasn't much money, especially on a missionary's salary, and what toys we got usually came via relatives in B.C. and Ontario. I seem to recall Christmas being a time when these items arrived, some of them repaired castoffs from cousins from somewhat wealthier families. Nonetheless, they were exciting to us. What they were I don't remember well, but they included small wagons and trucks, definitely no guns or weapons of any kind.

There was no television, and only the occasional static-filled shortwave radio which Dad listened to intently. One recollection still vivid some 60 years later is hearing Adolph Hitler (in German, I presume) ranting and raving and my Father saying something like "that man will bring us all to war." A year later he was in the army so it must have been Christmas 1938. Of course the King's (George VI) address was an absolute must, more important I think, to my mother than midnight mass.

Normally, in the winter, we played games at home with friends because of the Yukon's legendary cold. Chinese checkers seemed a regular and then Monopoly as we got a bit older. Cards were not allowed on Sundays (the favored game being "fish") and not much of anything else after Sunday School (where I learned my first, but not last, swear word) and two church services.

In more clement weather we played the usual kids' games: hopscotch, skipping, kick-the-can, tag, some rudimentary form of street hockey, and football, I guess. A favorite winter pastime was sliding down the banks of the slough behind our house on toboggans and sleighs. I recall well making myself a snow model of the inside of a car using tin cans as the dashboard, a stick for the gearshift, and something [else] for the steering wheel, and spending a lot of time pretending to be a truck driver.

I don't recall many games in the organized sense. Getting dressed to go to school in the winter was a chore, and the very short hours of daylight meant we were home a lot once school was out. I remember seeming to get endless little sets of watercolor paints with a brush or two in a tin case (which I was terrible at) and crayoning colouring books, all of which came from "outside" (i.e. the south!). We were encouraged to read a lot. All of the Thornton W. Burgess animal books are still vivid memories, and I think reading, both for pleasure and escape, have lasted for my lifetime.

We had a house dog called Tippy (a black cocker spaniel) whom I adored and who was killed by some stray huskies while I was away visiting another missionary family at an Indian (Aboriginal to be politically correct) village called Moosehide, a few miles from Dawson City. My favorite pastime there was, with the other kids, chasing rats with sticks around old abandoned houses and piles of wood. I liked being included as an equal with the Indian kids. We also played other games, but I'm not sure what they were, with the kids living at the Indian residential hostel next door to our home.

Jim McCullum recalls: I remember almost nothing [of life in the Yukon] except I had a tricycle that was my constant companion. The sidewalks in Dawson City were made of wood. On one side was the street, on the other deep ditches. I remember falling off my tricycle into the ditch and cutting my head. Great trauma!

I also have a picture of myself as a child of about four holding a small fish that I or someone else in my family had caught. I must have accompanied my father and brother on a fishing trip.

GROWING UP IN QUEBEC

Margaret Nichols's family lived in a flat in Montreal, but they spent their summers at Magog in the Eastern Townships of Quebec.

Games in the House

We played cards, but never on Sunday while our grandparents were there. Other games included Tiddly Winks, Pick up Sticks, Snakes and Ladders, and Parcheesi. We had a marble game related to Chinese Checkers that was a gift from Eaton's Department Store Santa. We also had a beautiful wooden Crokinole board with an inlaid design.

Another item was a 3D Viewer with a fascinating set of pictures that belonged to a friend.

Cork work—making things.

There were no libraries nearby, but we owned the important books. There were also comic books, colouring books, dot-to-dot books, "painting" with water and the colour appears (pretty uncreative) books.

We made scrap books, the early ones were made from greeting cards, Eaton's Catalogue pictures, etc. Later I made several Royal Family scrapbooks which I still have.

I played with dolls, and among my dolls was a black doll which, looking back, I find interesting for the 1940s. Her name was (what else) "Topsy." I also had two doll carriages, one of which was made of wicker.

We had a lot of paper dolls. We, especially my sister, made clothes for them. We each had a set of seventeen children of different ages who had names. (I still remember their names.)

Winter Games

We went skating in a local park. We played marbles, on packed snow, and collected hoards of them in the spring when the snow melted. We made Snow Angels and just played in the snow.

Summer Games in the City

We played active games like Kick the Can and Run Sheep Run. We had bolo Bats, yo-yos, and roller skates that were tightened on to our shoes. We threw a lacrosse ball against a wall while counting or reciting rhymes. We girls skipped, and the most complicated skipping patterns were done in grades 6 and 7.

Summer at the Cottage

Of course, we went swimming and we rowed out in a small boat built by my friend's father. We played "House" in the loft over the old stable at a local farm. Jumping into the hay mow was a favorite game.

Some things were fun for me although they were part of the duties of my contemporaries who lived on the farm. I enjoyed taking lemonade to the haying crew and (occasionally) riding on the rising pile of hay on the rick behind Dolly and Pete (the big farm horses).

At parties we played Pin the Tail on the Donkey, Button Button, Musical Chairs, and Remembering Objects on a Tray.

Radio

Radio was very much a part of our lives. We listened to children's programs, and later, to musical dramas and mysteries. A friend had a wind-up gramophone which was fun. We only got our first record player when I was 14.

Movies

Occasionally we would attend special Disney cartoon movies, but in Quebec attendance at "adult" movies was limited to those sixteen or more years old. By mid-high school we attended musicals. Of course, there were no drive-ins in Quebec.

War-Inspired Activities

In the 1940s the back of cereal boxes had, or to be sent for, various things like Morse code clickers, vanishing inks, codes, periscopes, etc. Carrying the Tools to Britain was a board game which involved moving materials west to east across Canada to Halifax (including uranium from Port Radium).

We did not have a TV until I was at university and won one as a prize (seat # drawn) at a McGill Carnival hockey night. By then I was too busy to watch very much but my parents enjoyed it and I left it with them. In my own family—we did not get one till Andy (our son) was about eleven.

THERE WERE LOTS OF PLAYMATES

Lis Schmidt Robert grew up in the town of Ponoka, Alberta. She recalls the games she and her friends played.

There were lots of kids to play with because they were all outside playing. Tenting blankets hung over the clothesline made a good house where we played house, dolls, school, or store. We made elaborate mud pies. We skipped. We learned to do spool knitting and embroidery work. We read the clouds and made patterns on frosted windows. We also enjoyed outside treasure hunts, especially at Easter when we could exchange the plaster of Paris egg we found for a chocolate one. (Chocolate is still my weakness.)

Other activities included playing in the sandbox, spinning a button on a string, marbles, jacks, Ante-I-Over, Run Sheep Run, Prisoner's Base and Kick the Can. Cops and Robbers, Cowboys and Indians, and Hide and Seek were perennial favorites. My dad made stilts and we walked around on those.

In the winter, of course, there were snowballs fights from [snow] forts—an activity now forbidden on Edmonton school grounds.

When there were enough children, we played baseball and hockey, and when there were not enough children, we played scrub (ball) and shinny (hockey). Biking, hiking, and arm wrestling were also fun. There were lots of board games and we Pinned the Tail on the Donkey at birthday parties. We also participated in Elocution Contests sponsored by the Women's Christian Temperance Union [WCTU]. And there were those times when we just sat around and talked—sometimes around a campfire.

Girls' hockey, Sweetwater School #1156, c. 1938.

Before a drainage system was installed, Ponoka experienced frequent spring floods. We often rafted about on sections of wooden sidewalks that had been broken off by the flood waters.

SPRING SPORT

Young Co-operators, *The Western Producer*
May 16, 1940

TWILIGHT

Dear Co-ops,

Every spring before the snow is quite gone we school-kids go out and start playing pump-pump-pull-away. It is about the only thing we think of all day. When the novelty wears off we argue about who's supposed to be it until half go off catching gophers and the other half decide there isn't time to have a decent game.

Finally we don't play anything for a couple of days. Then we get out last year's softball and mend it with a blunt needle and then argue about who is going to choose up. In the end we finally get started. Everything goes smoothly for a couple of days and the ball rips again. It isn't worth mending so we take off the outside and play with the inside. By the time noon hour is over there's only some small pieces of string left. Then we call a special Civic League meeting and move and second three or four motions and get a new ball.

Until the new ball comes we find another old ball and mend it up. The first day we have two balls we talk half the noon hour about whether we should wear out the old one, or soften up the new one. The new one is more of a novelty so we play with it. The first week we rarely play, just bat out flies because it hurts too much to catch the ball. And there's more than me knows it. Yours for more ball games.

SEEMS LIKE OLD TIMES

Helen Hansen grew up in 1940s Toronto.

"Why don't you go out and play?" my mother would say. It was more of a command than a question. And out I'd go, often with my prized India rubber ball in hand. Between our house and the neighbour's was a paved driveway, the perfect place to play ball. The neighbour's wall was a flat brick surface with no windows or chimney space jutting out. She must have been driven crazy with that constant pounding but never once asked me to stop. "Ordinary, moving, one hand, the other hand, one foot, the other foot," I'd chant aloud as I went through the lengthy routine, trying never to drop the ball because then I'd have to start all over again. If I did drop it, the ball would invariably roll down the sloping driveway and out onto the busy Toronto street where we lived. But we kids knew to be careful of traffic.

Playing with two balls was very difficult, but one became good at it with practice. I used softer spongy balls for that. They were red, blue, and white and, with wear, pieces would drop off them and expose the pale terra cotta colour within. The chant would be, "Gypsy, gypsy, lived in a tent. She had no money to pay her rent." Didn't realize the racist overtones.

Skipping was a favoured pastime, either with friends or alone. I had a wonderful rope, real rope, not plastic, that was long enough for Double Dutch. We'd count by twos until we tripped, "thirty, two, four, six, eight, forty, two four." Sometimes we'd just use a single, long rope and chant rhymes. This was easier than Double Dutch if there were little kids or boys who wanted to play. If there was no one out, I'd skip alone, winding the ends of the rope around my hands so many times the rope became large lumps on my fists.

Hopscotch was played in the driveway or on the school grounds. One of the kids would have a thick, stubby piece of chalk with which to draw the boxes for the game. It was important to find a good "man," the pebble that was used by a player. It had to be one that didn't roll but could be tossed into a box and would stay put.

"I borrows to be Roy Rogers!" "I borrows to be Dale Evans!" my friends would shout as we'd run out of the house to play Cowboys and Indians. I was always a bit dozy and would come last shouting, "I borrows to be Trigger!" This desire to pretend to be certain characters came from the movies. Saturday matinees at the Century Theatre at Broadway and Danforth in Toronto would feature double bills for kids. We'd watch Hopalong Cassidy and Gene Autrey, whose name we pronounces as Aw-ter-ee, and of course, the favourite, Roy Rogers. Every new film prompted hours of play as we galloped around hiding behind bushes and pouncing on each other. A piece of wood became a "gun," tie a hanky around your face and your were "the bad guy." We sang "Happy Trails To You" as we "rode off into the sunset."

I spent a lot of time on a farm up near Keswick, a village about fifty miles north of Toronto. The family there had a daughter my age. If we stayed close to the farmhouse, one or the other of her parents would find work for us to do, so we'd head out to the fields first thing in the mornings. As the farm had a hundred and fifty acres, there was plenty of territory to disappear into. At the beginning of the summer, it was necessary to search the fields for the newest, and cleanest (least important) cattle salt lick. Despite her father's admonition to "leave the salt lick alone," we'd go to find it, and, using a good-sized rock, would break off two corners and pocket them. All day, as we played, we'd take licks of the salt, carefully hiding them from grownup eyes. They'd last for weeks. Every time we'd fall and skin our knees and cry, our tears left white salt streaks down our cheeks. (Odd that we didn't later develop high blood pressure.)

Although I enjoyed playing with cut-out dolls, I rarely did so on my own. Another friend and I both loved to draw and colour and dreamed about becoming fashion designers when we grew up. The cut-outs were store-bought. But all of their clothing was designed by us. We'd talk constantly about the doll characters, where they were going and what they were doing, as we drew, coloured, and cut. Our parents kept us supplied with pads of plain paper. It was an easy way to keep us out of their hair for hours on end.

Other indoor activities included Chinese Checkers (I kept my marbles in an old snakeskin purse), which you could even play alone by making your move and then turning the board to the next "player." Pickup Sticks was a popular choice. Oh, how we'd argue whether or not a stick had moved! And there were always decks of cards handy for a game of Rummy or Crazy Eights. Canasta was perfect for those rainy summer days with the elderly woman in the cottage next door at Lake Simcoe.

When I was in kindergarten and came home at noon, my Mor (Danish for "mother") would have lunch ready. Her kitchen smelled of baking, and she'd give me a glass of milk and some chocolate chip cookies for dessert. Sounds like a cliche? Perhaps, but true nonetheless. And then I was allowed to turn on the radio in the kitchen and listen to "Ma Perkins." It was magic. A time to sit quietly and dream a little.

A "MULIGAN" ROAST

Pathfinders, *Free Press Prairie Farmer*
September 7, 1938

Olive Kastaskuk (13)
Vegreville, Alta.
*(Editor's Note — You must have very good humoured neighbours, Olive.
I am very afraid I would be pretty cross.)*

Dear Pathfinders,

I am going to tell you about a real muligan roast. We start when it is just getting dark and to everyone's horror (but ours) we actually take corn and potatoes out of other people's gardens. Of course every person expects their corn and potatoes to be raided. They are every year.

Then some of the gang run ahead and get heaps of wood and pile it real high, and then light it. We throw the potatoes in and then peel the corn. We keep the corn over the fire with green branches till the kernels pop. We take butter and salt and have a wonderful time eating corn around the blazing fire and telling stories. After the fire is just coals we take sticks and roll the potatoes out in the grass. They are very good with butter and salt.

I would like tons of correspondence. I save movie stars and my favorite movie stars are Henry Fonda, Judy Garland, Sonja Heine and Jane Withers. I would like to exchange favorites.

Creating Their Own Equipment

INSECT COLLECTION

Maple Leaf Club, *Family Herald and Weekly Star*
March 14, 1917

Evan Shute
NATURALIST
Idlerton, Ontario

Dear Maple Leaves—

I would like very much to be a Maple Leaf. I read your corner with much interest. I am eleven years old and going to Collegiate School.

I have a particular hobby—it is insect collecting. I am passionately fond of this, and spend most of my summer holidays adding to my collection. I only started a year ago, but I have over two hundred insects now.

Recently, a friend who went down to Jamaica to visit some friends, sent me some insects. I would be delighted if any Leaves would send me some, and I would return the favor in any way possible.

A MECHANICAL LEAF

Maple Leaf Club, *Family Herald and Weekly Star*
May 1, 1918

Simon Gaudet
HUNTER
Melbourne, Yar. County, N.S.

Dear Maple Leaves:

I live eight miles from town on a farm alone with my mother and father.

My favorite sports are hunting and riding horseback.

I made a windmill that can saw wood one inch in diameter. I also made a saw myself.

I have two pets, a dog and a cat, their names are Fanny and Mary Joe.

I would like to correspond with Leaves my own age, sixteen.

ENJOYS DOING FRETWORK

Pathfinders, *Free Press Prairie Farmer*
February 16, 1944

Danny Goosen (11)
[Address unclear]

Dear Pathfinders,

The boys in school do fretwork every Friday afternoon. We just started before Christmas so hadn't made many things yet. I made a toothbrush holder, name plate and elephant bookends. We'll be doing more of this work from now on. My brother has a fretwork saw which I take to school every Friday. I intend to have my own soon. My hobbies are doing fret work, bicycle riding and horseback riding. I'd like to have letters from boys my age who enjoy fretwork like myself.

BUILDING BOATS ALONG THE SKEENA

Used with permission from E.H. Harris, *Spokeshute: Skeena River Memory* (Victoria: Orca Books, 1990).

Boys are fascinated by boats and water. E.H. Harris and his Port Essington friends felt the call of the Skeena River.

Port Essington, like most other coastal settlements, was entirely dependent on boats. Although located at the tip of a peninsula it might just as well have been on an island, because every arrival and departure had of necessity to be by boat. When the area was known only as Spokeshute the crafts were all native dugout canoes, but after it became Port Essington there were rowboats, sailboats, tugboats, gasboats, sternwheelers, riverboats, and coastal steamboats, but there were no flying boats or other aircraft until after 1921.

Port Essington children soon became familiar, at least by sight, with all these vessels. Even before we were six years old Walter and Freddie Noel and I were building marvellous boats in our backyards from wooden packing cases. They looked wonderful there, with a sharp bow and pilot house built on to the box, and a steering wheel made from a lard pail lid that sometimes operated a rudder that really turned. If we occasionally filled all the cracks and lugged our boat down the steps, across Dufferin Street, and over the rocks to the shore, our illusions were always shattered. Our beautiful boat immediately took in water and became just a messed-up wooden box floating lopsidedly, awash in the river.

The only one who made a box boat that really floated was Jimmy Donaldson, who was a couple of years older and a lot more practical. Jimmy obtained a large box of the type used for packing whole salted spring salmon, about four feet long, two feet wide, and ten inches deep. He made the box watertight by nailing strips of wood over any open spaces and caulking all the seams. Two boards nailed together like an inverted letter V were attached to the front end to form a sharp bow. Jimmy then made holders for row locks, nailed a board across the box for a seat, cut down an old pair of oars to a convenient size, and his boat was ready to be launched. Unlike our impractical creations, Jimmy's salmon box boat, ugly duckling that it was, floated perfectly.

Jimmy manned the oars and I sat on a large rock in the stern to provide ballast. We went for a short row, close to the beach and around the piles of Frizzell's wharf. Except for the splashes from a few wavelets that wet the seat of my pants this sea trial was entirely successful. It is not surprising that when he grew up Jimmy Donaldson became a successful boatman.

As children we learned how to handle small boats sensibly, but we were also on a first-name basis with all the larger craft on the river.

BIRDS RETURNING

Pathfinder Page, *Free Press Prairie Farmer*
April 2, 1919

MARGARET DWYER (10)
Oak Point, Man.

Dear Pathfinders:

I had almost given up all hopes of writing. I have written six times and only saw one in print. Well, I hope the W.P.B. [waste paper basket] is asleep when this one goes by for he sure likes to take my letters. Spring is near. The horned lark and whiskey jack are back, and the crows will soon be coming. The blue-jay, Arctic owl, sparrows, and the wood-peckers stay here all winter. You may pick out the one you think is best and print it if you wish. My ambition now is to be when I am older a school-teacher. I like school well. I am ten and am in grade five. I own one pure Holstein calf. Her name is Mollie, and she is registered. I would like [some] merry person to write to me. I will answer all letters.

WHOOPIE TI YI YO!

Reprinted with the permission of Victor Carl Friesen and HSBC Bank
Canada. In *Pioneer News* 21, 3 (Fall 1998), published by the HSBC.

*Victor Carl Friesen dreamed of being a cowboy. His interest
was fostered by weekly funny papers, radio programs, books,
and movies.*

So I was a cowboy in my heart and mind, an ordinary individual
and defender of the right at home in the great outdoors, alive to
my surroundings and forward-looking. The world lay before me.

Being a "cowboy" affected my work, and everyday chores I
had to do, from chopping wood to gathering eggs, for I performed them with a self-reliance that made my parents proud,
they not knowing of my new-found sense of honor, my code of
the West. I was nothing daunted by whatever tasks fell to me.
Each presented "visions of unlimited possibilities." Carrying in
wood was a replenishing of the "campfire" in the kitchen range
(with Mother as camp cook). Collecting eggs was a scrounging
for food in a "vast treeless plain."

It was in my play, however, that my being a cowboy most
overtly affected my activities. For several months on end, I
walked about with a gun at my hip. It was wooden revolver of my
own carving (with a handle wrapped in hockey stick tape) fitted
into a black denim holster. The latter I asked my mother to sew for
me, and she also added a wide belt to which she had stitched a
row of spent cartridges from somebody's .32 calibre rifle.

My further accouterments included a high round-topped
farmer's straw hat, which I had soaked in water and reshaped to
flatten the crown, to give a Spanish aspect. To this end, too, I had
added a wide silk band and bent up the brim all around. Then I
had a colored handkerchief about my neck as a bandanna, and
one of Dad's old vests over my regular shirt and pants. The vest,
of course, was too big for me and did hang much below the belt
line of my usual trousers.

Sometimes, for show, I wore my older sister's trim rubber
boots under the pant legs. That footwear, I felt, had the appearance of a real cowboy boot that would fit well in a stirrup—if

only I had a saddle and, more importantly, if only I had a horse. Ah, well…

Dad supplied the final item of my outfit—a rope. It was a new one and, full of twists, would not coil smoothly. I remember soaking it in a tub of water and then circling it between two posts to take the kinks out of it. Then, since I had found a brass "eye" among some old junk, this was spliced into it to give a genuine lariat or lasso. I used it for letting myself down from the barn loft, where I sometimes slept as though I were a hired hand.

The Spanish words "lasso" and "lariat" had a nice Western sound to my ear and, dressed in my assembled outfit, I used them *pronto* on all occasions. I also bolstered my vocabulary with Spanish terms like *remuda, arroyo* and *sombrero* and particularly liked that language's names for kinds of horses—*pinto* and *palominos*.

When one of my cousins, another "cowboy," came for a visit, we would ride the range together, horseless, running about like loping horses, playing Cowboys and Rustlers among the willow clumps of our pasture, our log smokehouse being the guardroom or jail for lawbreakers. We practised lassoing fence posts, drawing guns from holsters, and rounding up dogies. *Whoopie Ti Yi Yo!*

INFECTED BY A RADIO BUG

Rolland Lewis recalls life in the Point Grey district before it became part of Vancouver.

On a number of occasions I have somewhat facetiously remarked that I had the good sense to be born into a "comfortable" Point Grey family. My father was a small employer, about 20 employees at the peak of his business, in an industry which held up well when I was a child during the Depression years. Consequently, I had a secure, stable upbringing. During my young years, I did the usual boyhood things, such as play cowboys and Indians, build model boats, and play "scrub." The content of our weekly play was often determined by the nature of the Saturday afternoon matinee for kids at the local theatre.

Not until about age 11 did I begin to seriously make my own fun. About that time I was bitten by what was called the "radio bug," and from that age onward a considerable part of my spare time went toward "radio." Very quickly I learned the code, and practised it regularly with two of my friends who were also interested in radio. We built our own crystal sets, scrounging and adapting parts as required, and communicated locally in code using Ford spark coils run by whatever used dry cells we could acquire. This was highly unlawful, but we did not know this at the time.

Patricia and Rolland Lewis on a family fishing trip to Big Barr Lake, BC, c. 1930.

As one can imagine, this led to some interesting situations. When we used our spark coils as transmitters, they covered all radio frequencies for several blocks about our houses. Naturally, this interfered with broadcast radio reception, and although our neighbours were not sure of the cause, it did not stop them from accusing us kids of ruining their reception. One day my friend who lived across the back lane and I gathered all the old wire we could find, strung it between our houses, and hooked up earphones so we could talk. We did this the day that King George V died and the local radio stations ceased broadcasting in respect for the deceased king. Our phone rang all afternoon with the neighbours demanding that we take down our wire IMMEDI-ATELY as it had cut off their radio reception!

At age 14 I passed my Department of Transport exam, and became an active amateur radio operator. From that time on my friends and I built legitimate radio transmitters and receivers, often from scrounged, begged, traded, or adapted used parts, and talked with other hams all over the world. But the real fun days were those before we became licensed amateurs, when we built our crystal sets and spark coils.

A RADIO MADE FROM A RAZOR BLADE

When young John Fedoruk found instructions for building simple radios, he began making his own.

One of the fun things to do when I was a boy was to make your own radio. Although I did not know how a radio worked I knew they did work. I built a number of them and listened to a number of the local radio stations. I did not have much tuning capacity so I was stuck with whatever the local station had on. For an antenna I used the clothesline and for ground I used a metal rod pounded into the ground. It was forty-five years later that I became a HAM, and you know I am still trying to figure out how radio works.

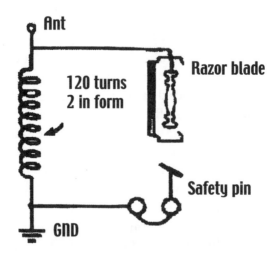

Razor Blade Radio, *QST*, 1944. Reprinted with permission of Steve Ford, Editor, *QST*.

ALONE BUT NOT LONELY

Marilyn Diane Duncanson Barker grew up on the family farm near London, Ontario.

Even when I became old enough to go to school, there were no other children living on the farms in the mile between our house and the one-room school. It therefore will become apparent that I spent much time alone, or with my parents, grandparents, or my all-knowing responsive dog, Rover, who would run and jump with me, roll over, or do whatever was commanded. I remember throwing a rubber ball against our two storey brick house and seeing how high I could throw against the wall and how far back I could stand and still catch the ball. When I got a wagon, I had to learn to kneel on the wagon with one knee and to push with the other foot while I steered. Learning to ride my new blue bicycle with balloon tires was frustrating until I got the knack of balancing, for it required an adult to run behind steadying me as I rode. I remember humming and singing a lot just to hear a voice and even talking aloud as I imagined elaborate stories happening as I watched the ever-changing patterns in the clouds. I had the usual little-girl playthings such as dolls and a doll carriage. How I loved a new colouring book, new pencils, and a box of eight new crayons! I loved nursery rhymes, Mother Goose stories, etc., but I wasn't satisfied until I could decipher the words for myself. That same determination led me to plead with and pester my mother until she shared her talents with me—sewing, knitting, crocheting, and embroidery work. When my Aunt Kay, a high school Latin and French teacher, visited for holidays, she allowed me to play dress-up with her wonderful array of clothes and shoes. My mastery of French phrases grew and grew as the years went by also. Another school teacher aunt taught me the art of scrapbooking by theme at an early age. I remember *Life* magazine being a favourite source of pictures that I could clip and glue once my aunt had mixed me some flour and water paste. I liked to visit my other set of grandparents because they had a swing set, and it was at their house that I learned to pump by myself.

After I started school, I spent endless hours at home copying my notebooks, trying to produce beautiful writing and illustrat-

ing pages where appropriate. We had Mission Band and Junior
Red Cross meetings once a month and with one of these organizations came a children's magazine. I longed for the next issue
so I could find a new pen pal in some far away place. Many
hours were spent at home writing letters on airmail paper. At
school I learned skipping rhymes, how to play hopscotch, dodge
ball, Simon says, Red light-green light, frozen tag, and regular
tag, and to blow the ripened dandelion heads to scatter the
seeds, and to pick wild daisy petals from the flowers as I recited,
"He loves me, he loves me not."

Our teacher put together fine Christmas concerts for which
we rehearsed our lines weeks in advance. We took great pride in
our final performance. She taught us to square dance and to perform musical drills. She arranged for whole skating afternoons
on a farmer's pond where all forty of us would skate till our toes
stung from the cold. Choosing sides for baseball games was fun
because every single person got to be on a team regardless of
size or skill. Spelling bees were my favourite team sport because
I found that at a very early age I could spell better than the big
grade eight boys. I loved the new books that came with the travelling library. Someone, probably an older student, taught me
how to make origami creations.

My parents organized much of my socializing. Ballet, tap and
highland dancing, baton twirling, piano and organ lessons led me
to all kinds of associations with people: sleepovers with giggling,
participation in community garden parties, and school shows. I
have a photo to prove my part in a 150th church anniversary in our
Scottish community. A local playwright wrote a humorous historical play in which I danced the Highland Fling. My first experience
horse-back riding occurred at the farm of one of my dancing
friends. My first introduction to a camp came with an invitation
from another dancing friend to accompany her family for a weekend as they prepared to open a CGIT camp for the season.

Although there was a lot of work for everyone on the farm, I
particularly delighted in the afternoons spent with my grandfather playing board games while the rest of the family did their
shopping and banking in the city — Crokinole, Parcheesi, Chinese Checkers, Snakes and Ladders. Later, my uncle who visited

the farm taught me to play cribbage. There were picnics, walks to the woods, wild berry picking, trips on the London and Port Stanley railway, riding the incline railway at Port Stanley, and frolicking on the beach. On one visit I managed to get the autograph of Ray Anthony, the band leader.

Many of the adults' pleasant pastimes eventually became mine. For example, no one ever left our community without knowing how to play euchre. I particularly liked anything social — even the visits from "the Raleigh man," a smiley friendly gentleman who spoke with such a smooth voice as he extolled the virtues of pure vanilla. I liked harvest time when our kitchen would be filled with the aroma of fresh homemade pies, hungry men, stories, and laughter. Spring brought visits from Steve Newhouse and his family, Indians who lived on the Munsey Indian Reservation who helped my father harvest his one and one-half acres of strawberries each year.

Then there was that fine line between work and play. On the farm I was expected to work hard, but there were those jobs I chose to do which seemed to be fun for me — washing the car, weeding flower beds, polishing silver, collecting sap from maple trees for maple syrup making, and learning to paint woodwork with a real paint brush.

I find it interesting that there is such a strong link between the pleasurable activities of my childhood and the ones I enjoy as an adult. Is it all that surprising that I am a calligrapher, a quilter, a knitter, a scrapbooker, and a gardener, that my husband and I have theatre and symphony subscriptions, and that we enjoy card games, and that I still like writing letters?

IT WAS A MAGICAL TIME

Audrey Kendall recalls her childhood on a Saskatchewan farm as a happy busy time.

For the first thirteen years of my life I lived on a farm near McNutt in eastern Saskatchewan. I don't recall feeling deprived at the lack of siblings. Every day was packed with activities that

I considered fun. In the winter after school, my dog, Rover, and I would haul snow and wood to the house. I would grind grain and make mash for my ducks and pet my favorite, Sir Francis. I would gather the eggs and talk to my special hens. Occasionally, my father would tow me on my skis behind the horse-drawn sleigh. At school we would play fox and goose, make snow forts, and have snowball fights. During bad weather we would play indoors—tag, board games, blackboard games, and cards. At home after supper my father and I would play cards or board games or put together jigsaw puzzles. My favorite games were Rummy, Parcheesi, Mill, and Crokinole played on our home-made board. Our dogs would be curled up on the couch and I would join them while reading a book from the school library. On many evenings my mother taught me needlecrafts and baking.

Springtime would bring the flooded creeks and sloughs. I would wade in the water, build dams, and chase after the wild ducks who would use the broken-wing technique to lure me away from their nests. I would frequently go to the highest point on our farm—Crocus Hill—to see the wild flowers, at first white and purple crocuses and later cowslips, shooting stars, lady slippers, bluebells, and wild roses. At school, springtime meant playing hopscotch, skipping rope, softball, and track and field. One year we had a teacher who taught us how to play cricket. That was a lot of fun. Games like "Kick-the-Can," "Stealing the Wickets," "Red Rover, Come Over," "Prisoner's Base," "Tag," "Ball-on-the-Roof," Anti-i-over," and "Hide-and-Seek" kept us well entertained at school recesses and lunch hours. At home there would be chores: feeding the young chicks, goslings, ducklings, baby turkeys, calves, lambs, and occasionally, a foal. My dogs and I would fetch the cows for milking and haul wood and water to the house. I would help my mother plant and later weed the garden. Although these tasks were really work, I thought of them as entertainment. Only housework was considered work.

Summer holidays meant gathering the vegetables from the garden and helping my mother can them. Our farm had wild strawberries, raspberries, pincherries, chokecherries, gooseberries, saskatoons, hazelnuts, and a few high-bush cranberries. Berry picking and eating was great fun. Again, I would help my mother preserve these fruits and nuts for winter enjoyment. Occasionally, my cousins and I would meet and play ball and other outdoor games. Every church parish would have a picnic and that meant hot dogs, ball games, and races. In a dry summer my father and I would go by horse-drawn wagon to the deep willow-ringed pond to fetch water for garden use. This was one of my favorite activities.

Autumn brought harvest time. My father allowed me to play in the grain as the granaries were being filled, and I helped my mother take food and drinks out to the threshers in the fields for their coffee breaks.

For my parents, life on the farm was very hard and I later realized they had many worries and concerns, but for me, then, it was a magical time.

TRY CRAB-APPLE PIE

Young Co-operators, *The Western Producer*
October 16, 1941

Ever a Co-op,
HOLLYHOCK (14)
Bowden, Alta

Dear Young Housekeepers—

I've picked so many chokecherries for jelly and eaten so many I feel like a chokecherry myself, but that wouldn't interest you.

I know something that will, though. Have you ever tried making crab-apple pie? It takes a little more sugar, but boy! it's good. You just wash and core the crabs, don't peel 'em. Sprinkle with spices and mix a little more sugar in with them than you use with ordinary apples.

I hope you like it.

I MADE MY OWN TOYS

Glen Sullivan recalls using his father's tools to create his own toys and equipment.

I am seventeen years younger than my brother and six years younger than my sister, consequently I was reared very much as a single child. Much of my early play was by myself. My father, who was in his early fifties when I was born, was a busy man but he often took a few minutes to show me how to do something and never got upset at finding me in the workshop using his basic tools. I learned to handle these by watching him repair equipment or make objects that were needed around the farm.

Between ages three and seven, my efforts focused on the making of plows by using a piece of tin to make the moldboard. This was then nailed to a piece of board. I spent many hours playing in the dirt making furrows and then using a board with nails in it to act as a harrow. I still remember the wet morning when Father was in the shed and I collected some sticks of firewood which he cut crosswise into slabs. I spent hours making tractors, using the slabs for wheels.

I used available scrap pieces of half-inch pipe to make toy guns. My greatest kick was the day Father used the front wheels from an old grain binder, a piece of pipe, a cog wheel with a crank handle, and a strip of tin, to make a machine gun which made a lot of noise when the crank handle was turned.

My winters were spent playing in the hay shed or the hay loft. My only companion was my dog who followed me everywhere. He enjoyed a game of tug-of-war with me and he was always the winner. This was pure joy for him as he would sometimes bring the rope to me.

In the years between seven and twelve my world expanded a great deal. I had more contact with other children through school and with the neighbours' children who lived nearby, but I still had to rely on my own imagination a great deal.

Making tractors was replaced by the manufacture of sling shots, bows and arrows, stilts using two poles with right-angle blocks to stand on, darts made from old cedar shingles, and a thrower made with a stick and string. I was overjoyed one day when I found an old saddle and the barrel from an old shotgun that had been thrown away when a family moved. The saddle ended up on a fence rail and it became a horse. The gun barrel ended up with a stock traced from father's shotgun. The only manufactured toys I remember receiving were a Meccano set, a top, a windup train, a bolo bat, a cap gun and holster, and skis. The rest of my toys I made myself.

Springtime was the time for making rafts from old telephone poles and for catching tadpoles. Wintertime was spent playing in the hay loft and working with my Meccano set in the living room. I remember that the snow was deep those winters and travel was difficult, so I made several pairs of snowshoes using the sides of old apple boxes and pieces of rope.

By this point I was bigger and stronger and the tug-of-war with the dog had progressed to my swinging the dog through the air as he held on to the end of the rope.

One summer our neighbour had a dugout (watering pond) excavated for his cattle. His son and I spent many hours rolling down the hill of dirt into the bottom of the dugout in his red wagon.

Between ages thirteen and seventeen I progressed to using a .22 rifle and shotgun. The sparrow population in the barn and graneries declined rapidly. And summer afternoons were spent rowing a flat-bottom boat on the neighbour's large slough. When autumn came the boat was used when duck hunting.

I became quite handy with hammers, saws, and other tools, and I made weather vanes in the shape of biplanes with propellers that spun in the wind. These were given to anyone who wanted one.

I spent one Easter holiday turning the handle of the blacksmith forge while my father sharpened the teeth on the field harrows. I saw how he worked steel using heat. To try out my own skills I chose a piece of water pipe and had a try at making copies of some spears a friend's father had sent back from Africa. Unfortunately, the spear broke the first time I threw it.

The 4H Baby Beef Calf Club became part of my life and I began to spend my time on more serious things. I can still identify the best beef animal in the herd.

As a child I spent a lot of time playing alone, but I can't say that I was ever the victim of boredom.

SEEPEETZA GETS A DOLL

Shirley Sterling, *My Name Is Seepeetza* (Vancouver: Douglas and McIntyre, 1982).

Shirley Sterling provides a glimpse into life in an Indian residential school. There were toys, activities, and playmates, but Seepeetza longed for the security of her home and her family.

Thursday, November 20, 1958, K.I.R.S.

I buried the doll today. Somebody from town gave the school some old dolls, and Sister gave one to me. It had a hard face and messy brown hair. Its eyes could open and close. It had eyelashes. Sister looked mad when she gave the dolls out, like it was a nuisance. Then she told us to go outside and play. The wind was blowing and I was so cold my hands felt numb. I went on the other side of the teeter-totters where there is soft sand, and I dug a hole and put the doll in it and covered it up so it would be safe from the cold.

My mum made me a doll once, a rag doll. She made it out of scraps on her sewing machine. It had yellow flowers on it. Then Missy wanted it so Mum gave it to her and made me another one. It had black and white stripes and I didn't like it. Anyway I'm too busy for dolls at home. I have to help my dad with the horses and everything.

After I buried the doll I looked up and saw this grade eight girl called Maryann watching me. She said she was a grandmother, and she had *stsa-wen*. I was surprised to hear her say that word. It means dried fish. I thought only we knew that word from home. She handed me an old dried piece of pine wood and told me to sit on the ground to eat my *stsa-wen*. We sat cross-legged on the ground facing each other near an old log so we could keep warm. The tumbleweeds were rolling past and the wind was kind of moaning.

Sometimes when it's cold we make tumbleweed houses or find a big cardboard box at the incinerator, climb inside and close the flaps. It's nice because we can keep warm and tell stories. When it's warmer out we play Auntie Auntie I Over with a rubber ball at the pump house. It's a little red hut with water pipes and a water pump. We throw the ball over it and run round to try and catch it on the other side. There are swings and a merry-go-round and teeter-totters in the playground, but I don't like them. They make me dizzy.

It's my cousin Mickey's fault I get dizzy because he gave me some chewing tobacco once when we were waiting in the truck outside the beer parlour for my dad. My dad came whistling around the corner and started up the truck at the same time I put some in my mouth. The smell of the gas and the taste of the snoose made me sick to my stomach. I fell down at the back of the truck and spat it out but the taste stayed for a long time. To this day I get car sick. I get sick on swings. I get sick tumbling in gym class.

Maryann surprised me by talking Indian. We're not supposed to. She ordered me to eat all my fish just like she was a real grandmother. We laughed. "I wish it was really fish," she said. "And I wish I was home with my grandmother. My parents are dead." She asked me if we ate salmon too. I nodded. The she whispered, "Sister is coming." We threw away the wood and jumped up and started running in because Sister was ringing the bell for supper.

Village Island children rowing out to meet the M.V. *Columbia II*, undated. The Columbia Collection, The Anglican Synod of British Columbia.

Animals: Friend, Foe, or Food

HUNTING GOPHERS IN SASKATCHEWAN

Harold Zwick grew up on a farm near Ryerson, Saskatch-ewan, where he and his brothers perfected the art of gopher hunting.

Charlie Riley's Pasture for Gopher Shoots

Charlie Riley's pasture was a favourite place for the young Zwick boys to catch prairie gophers. The hot summer sun on the prairies always brought the gophers out to sun themselves. The prairie gopher is a golden brown creature about seven inches long, a burrowing animal that loves to stand upright on his haunches beside his burrow with his body pointed straight up while surveying his neighbourhood. The prairie gopher squeaks when frightened and scurries about to gather his family and dash down his hole to apparent safety.

The Zwick's Ryerson farmhouse was on a slight knoll on Section 3, Township 10, Range 33, west of the 1st Meridian in Saskatchewan. The dining and living rooms of the isolated farmhouse both faced the south, about two hundred yards from the dirt road separating our farm from Charlie Riley's pasture. Hence on warm, sunny summer days we could see dozens of gophers from our dining room table as they played near their burrows.

This often inspired a summer afternoon of fun and marksmanship, since during lunch someone would shout "see all them gophers out there today!" That was usually all it took for Edward or Walter or one of the other older boys (on Sunday when they had time off) to say, "Mom, I'm going to shoot gophers for Walter's pet hawk," and we boys would gang up behind whomever got down the family 0.22 caliber weapon from its nail rack above the door in the hallway between the dining room and the washroom. The gun was always loaded with about 10 rounds of "longs" (purchased from Gerald Sandel at the Maryfield Hardware on Saturday night) in case a chicken-stealing fox or coyote appeared, so there was no need to waste time finding bullets.

Off we went to shoot gophers. This involved trying to sneak up within range (about 50 yards or less) so that the shooter had a realistic chance of hitting the 1.5" wide and 5 inches tall vertical target using the simple iron sights of the Cooey bolt-action rifle. I preferred the well-worn single-shot Winchester .22 rifle, probably because I was the youngest Zwick with least influence, and no one else wanted that old gun. That was the same reason I preferred the 410-gauge single-shot shotgun for duck hunting since the rounds were too expensive for gophers. In a large family you quite naturally learn to work with (and love) whatever small blessings you are allowed to get your hands on.

The Pinsonneault children in a wheat field, Gravelbourg, SK, undated (Saskatchewan Archives Board [R-A19540]).

A Gopher Bite at Sorenson's Farm

Another method of "catching" gophers (a misnomer really since the object was to kill them) was to "drown them out." Drowning out gophers is a skill learned by all prairie farm boys. The principle is simple, though the technology and timing require some degree of precision.

To drown out a gopher we would watch which burrow a gopher goes into and rapidly force him to re-emerge by flushing a large quantity of water down the hole after him. It is necessary to be reasonably quick, since the gopher may block his hole to keep the water out if he is given sufficient time and if he senses a water threat.

The trickiest part of the enterprise is the capture itself, since the gopher is quick and will not pause when he rockets from the watery hole. A strategy that often works is to have a ring of boys at the burrow entrance which causes the creature to momentarily pause with only his head out of the hole while he surveys the lay of the land and formulates his escape plan. It is at this moment that the well-prepared farm boy jerks on his binder twine noose, carefully placed around the burrow entrance. This jerk should garrotte the gopher and chalk one up for the farm boy.

An alternate or backup strategy is to have the farm dog (Sport, the border collie, in the case of our family) close at hand so that should the gopher bolt without a pause as he emerges from his burrow, or should the snare mechanism fail, then chalk one up for good old Sport.

One day when Edward and I were drowning out gophers at Sorenson's farm with our nephews Don and Ron, the gopher snare failed, and Sport was away studying a squirrel elsewhere on the farm, so I, in a split second when one must act or the whole enterprise fails, made the rash decision to grab the hesitant gopher with my bare hands. It was a successful but short capture, both the gopher and me squealing simultaneously, the gopher in fright and me in pain as the blood from his bite gushed from my finger. Chalk one up for the gopher.

Sport, Our Hunter Dog

Sport loved the chase of gophers. We needed to restrain him as he wedged his nose deep into the burrow, sniffing loudly and then drawing back to begin an always unsuccessful "dig," causing clumps of dirt to fly almost 25 yards out between his hind legs. And the snarling and occasional vicious bark! The poor gopher should have died of soul-numbing terror. However, Sport was not a great squirrel hunting dog, since he became frustrated at the chattering of a bushy tailed squirrel as it descended deep into one of the several rock piles at the edges of farm fields. My brothers and I would try to scare the cowering beastie by pretending we were removing all of his protective rocks, causing Sport to grow excited with the anticipation. Sport was envisioning a tender gray squirrel emerging at rocket speed, but the squirrel continued to chatter louder as we crashed rocks about and shouted. The blood curdling and vicious growls from Sport were inspiring and caused sweat to drop from eager boys' faces, but this was a hunt which I can not recall ending in any success, ever.

Money in Gopher Tails

Gopher tails and crows' eggs were worth money in those days. The "government" empowered the schoolteacher to pay two cents per gopher tail, two cents per crow's egg, and five cents per pair of crow's legs. Sounds like easy money, you say? We thought so, and eagerly ran off in all directions to spot crows nests to climb up to and rob along the road from home to school. And after school there were the gopher hunts.

I have difficulty recalling that the money ever amounted to more than enough to purchase a couple of chocolate bars. But more memorable than money were the old syrup tins of stinky gopher tails and crows legs jumbled in the bottom, together with "ripe" crows' eggs that some kids were simple enough to keep without "blowing" them out. The teacher surely earned her wages in those years.

VERY SPECIAL FRIENDS

Ken Strong recalls a very special adventure of his childhood.

As the 1940s turned into the 1950s I was a child of a poor family living on the Victoria waterfront. I mention this for a couple of reasons. First, even though I was thirteen, I was referred to as a "child" as advertising agencies had not yet developed the use of the term "teenager." Second, the old pre-1930s uninsulated summer cottages along the waterfront were home to many people in our struggling financial circumstances. (These cottages would be torn down later to make way for new housing.)

The memory that stands out, and which I share with you, did not cost a cent, but the action would be illegal today. A friend of better financial means than I had a ten-foot clinker boat which we would take out in all kinds of weather. During the summer of 1950 we were out every day, raking herring, spearing halibut, and just motoring or rowing around. Sometime during the summer a group of three porpoises, living just outside the bay, began to swim beside our boat. As time went on they moved in closer and closer until they were within arm's length, and just stayed motionless beside us. After we became accustomed to such familiarity, they started a game. One would swim rapidly at the boat and at the last minute duck under the boat and come up on the other side, then lie back and look at us with what seemed to be a smile on its face. This went on for several days, and then the rules changed. They would get out in front of us and we would go full tilt at them until, at the last minute, they would duck under the boat and come up, placing themselves for our next run.

We became good friends, to the point that if we were late getting out of the bay they would come looking for us. This continued for several weeks. But one afternoon while we were playing "chicken" with them, the two smaller ones took off. The big one made several attempts, using his nose, to push our boat back into the bay. Once we got the idea and headed in, he disappeared, too. Right then several killer whales appeared around the point. I never saw the porpoises again, but the free fun we had and the friendship we developed made that summer of 1950 into a very special summer. Of course, today it is illegal to approach sea mammals as the "powers that be" have decided we are interfering with them and they would rather be left alone. Yeah, right!

A YOUNG SPORTSMAN

Maple Leaf Club, *Family Herald and Weekly Star*
May 26, 1909

Fred J. Bicknell (15)
Barclay Siding, P.O., Ont.

Dear Maple Leaves:

Although I have been a member of this Club for several years, this is my first letter to the Leaves. I live in New Ontario not far from a couple of lakes, where there is pretty good fishing during the summer months. Big game is not very plentiful around here, but there is good sport for us boys in the fall, shooting partridges and rabbits. In the spring there is a little lake that melts and floods the marsh, and then the fish come up to the surface and are easily caught.

If some of the boys do not soon write, the girls will have the Club entirely to themselves. I would like to correspond with members of my own age.

Wishing all success to the Club.

FOND OF HUNTING

Maple Leaf Club, *Family Herald and Weekly Star*
September 24, 1909

Arthur Kay
ENGLISH LAD
Box 103, Jenner, Alta.

Dear Maple Leaves:

I am very fond of fishing and hunting. I always look for the month of September so as to watch my father shoot ducks and geese.

We are about one hundred and fifty yards from Cut Bank Lake. The lake is about a mile wide and two miles long. There are lots of rushes in the lake so it's hard to get the ducks without a boat.

Last winter I caught one hundred and eighty-one muskrats.

I would like to correspond with anyone my own age, 12.

OUR DUCK HUNT

Pathfinders, *Free Press Prairie Farmer*
January 2, 1924

Lloyd Essex (12)
Colfax, Sask.

Dear Pathfinders:

I have not had the pleasure of joining this jolly club before. My story is about a duck hunt which a pal and I had this fall. I had a .22 repeater, and my friend had a shotgun. We started out about 5 o'clock in the morning. We soon came to a slough and shot eight ducks. I fired five shots and got four ducks. Fred shot three times and got four also. We cooked two for our dinner. About a half an hour after dinner we went to another slough. It was about 4½ miles away. Here we got three more ducks. I shot two of these and Fred shot one. Well, I think I must close now. Good-bye.

BUNNY FOR A PLAYMATE

Pathfinders, *Free Press Prairie Farmer,* n.d.

Everett Sharpe (13)
Meskanaw, Sask.

Dear Pathfinders,

I am going to tell you about a pet rabbit I once had. I found him when my brother and I were getting wood. It was just a little baby rabbit then, and the horse we had nearly stepped on it. So I took it home and fed it. It would drink milk and water and eat bread, potatoes, grass, bark and any weeds he could get. He soon became a real pet and would run and play with the baby. If he got hungry and we didn't feed him he would follow us around until we would feed him. We had him for a long time. In the winter he would turn white and in the summer he would turn grey. One day he was playing and went outside, the dog began to chase him. We called the dog back, but it frightened the rabbit so much that he ran away and never came back again. I was very sorry to lose my poor little pet. I once had an owl for a pet but he died. I have a picture of him sitting on a chair. Hoping to receive letters from any boy my age.

A WONDERFUL PONY

Pathfinder Page, *Free Press Prairie Farmer*
April 21, 1920

Hazel M. Buckler (11)
Harptree, Sask.

Dear Pathfinders:

I want to tell you of the fun we had today. Oh! it was fun. Papa got us a dear little Shetland pony, a year and a half old, not broken in a bit.

Papa said he would get us harness and a cart, but we couldn't wait, so we got binder string from the straw stack, braided ropes, and made harness, using a pair of papa's braces for a breast strap. Then we hitched our pony, Minny, to our toboggan, and off she went. She went fine. Oh! it was fun. We went to our neighbor's and gave Pearl and Mervin a ride.

They said come again with that outfit. Then Minny came home with us, trotting along very nicely. Mamma and papa watched us from the window.

How they did laugh and wished they had the camera ready. We do love our little pony Minny.

I would like some girl of my own age to write to me. I will answer.

FEEDING THE BIRDS

Maple Leaf Club, *Family Herald and Weekly Star*
July 10, 1918

Richard Asher
LONECLIFFE
Vernon, B.C.

Dear Maple Leaves:

We have a good view of the Okanagan lakes and some other lakes near here.

I am ten years old and I am a member of the Audubon Society and I have been for a year.

I have built bird boxes and feeding tables and the birds are quite tame.

I am in the junior fourth reader and would like to correspond with any members of the Audubon Society.

JOTTINGS FOR MY FAMILY

Laurena Saunders shares her memories of life on a farm near Gregg, Manitoba.

My sisters, six and seven years older than I, were off at school, so I spent a lot of time on my own. I didn't care much about dolls, but I loved the cats and dog. I had a special cat, "Snooky" that allowed me to dress him and I would put him in the blue wicker doll buggy. I even had a bottle with a nipple for him. I was very sad when Snooky disappeared one spring. I suppose a wild animal—wolf or such—may have got him. I also had a chinchilla rabbit named "Nipper."

The farm animals were an important part of my life. We had small calves in our barn. One was resting quietly in the straw, so I decided it would be a nice place to sit so I sat square on the animal's back. It soon jumped up and I fell face down in the gutter. Yuk!! I went howling to the house. Mother couldn't stop laughing, but in short order soap and water were administered and I was as good as new. So much for that experience.

Janet and Beth Emslie with Tamas, c. 1940.

It was in the barn loft that I would find mother cat tenderly caring for her newborn kittens. She would purr loudly as she licked the babies. It was also in the barn that Mother and Dad allowed me another life experience—that of seeing a calf born. I think I was six or seven at the time. It all seemed very natural and normal and the scrawny wet calf was soon standing on its own feet. I guess my parents wondered what my response would be, but when they asked me, I recall saying, "It just came out," whereupon they sort of shook their heads. I guess, to me, it was just part of the way things were supposed to be.

The horses, cows, and sometimes the pigs, were sheltered in the barn. I spent a lot of happy time watching them. I would pat the cows as I could go along the alley in front of them, but I couldn't do that with the horses. I held them in awe; they were so big. They were work horses—one team was Jessie and Jeff, the other was Doll and Bill. We had a colt we named Prince. His mother was Maud. We never named the cows except for their colours—Reddy, Blacky, Roany, etc.

As I grew older, watching my Mom and others milk cows fascinated me. The barn cats eagerly watched too, as there was always a big dish of warm milk for them. Sometimes they would even sit on their hind legs while a stream of milk was squirted at them right from the source. Finally, I was allowed to try my hand at milking. The gentlest cow was chosen, and she was patient with me. But it wasn't as easy as it looked.

We had a gramophone and I would sit by it and play records. I remember one [record] about a train wreck, and also one about a fellow finding a rip in his pants when he was at a party. There were also nice marches and hymns, and the song "I Love Little Pussy." I had a bag of pennies and I remember listening to the music and counting my money. I also liked to visit Aunt Janey's house, because there was a homemade Noah's Ark complete with standup wooden animals.

Some of my happiest memories have to do with mud pies. I would set up my "kitchen" out by the wood pile—lots of blocks of wood were used to invent tables, chairs, stoves, etc. Mud would be mixed for cakes and ashes would be mixed for the icing, and all the while I could sing as loud as I wanted. It was the rule at our place—no shouting or yelling indoors.

My years at Dempsey (rural) School were happy ones. We were like a big happy family and we had a good time at recess.

Football was the game of winter, and we played softball in the summer. In June the school field day was held in Carberry. There, along with quite a number of other district schools, we would march behind our school banners to the fair grounds. The competition events were followed by a picnic lunch with our parents. It was always a great day of sunburns. Of course we had school "yells." I don't know who invented this one:

Zip Boom Bah
DEMPSEY DEMPSEY
RA RA RA
We've got the guts, we've got the grits
Nothing's Beaten Dempsey yet.
DE-M-P-SE-Y
DEMPSEY!

The biggest event of the winter was the Christmas concert. How we looked forward to it! When we were attending school in the country we practised our parts for the concert at the school, but for the final rehearsal the teacher would walk us the ¾ of a mile to the church, and there we would try to do everything right.

The big night would come—what excitement! I can almost smell the stately tree that had been erected. Some tinsel had been put on the branches. The gifts that the parents put on for their children and friends were, for the most part, the decorations, as there were no lights or gaudy ornaments. I remember I got a doll that had been hung on the tree for me. The boughs were strong and sturdy and accommodated the parcels as well.

After we had sung our last song and given our last skit there was a HO HO HO and a fat man in a red suit would arrive, right from the North Pole! Excitement couldn't have been higher. Then home we would go in the open sleigh and snuggle happily in our beds.

The next big event was Christmas Day at Grandma's. We always hung up our stocking on a clothesline stretched across the kitchen—we did not have a fireplace. Early in the morning we would come downstairs and unload the special treats. There were always some nuts, a few hard candies, and a Japanese orange in each stocking. There would be a few small items—soap, hankies, a game—but whatever it was it was JUST what we wanted. The radio would be on and the King (George V) would be speaking and there would be messages from the Commonwealth Nations that were from all parts of the world—India, Australia, etc. I can still recall the thrill of thinking we belonged to such a great group of nations—our "big family." How patriotic I felt!

Shortly after breakfast we put on our good clothes, and if we happened to have something new we knew it would be warm. When we were all outfitted with hats, scarves, mitts, boots, etc., we were ready. Then some would shout, "He's here!" Sure enough, Dad, with a team of horses (all decked with jingle bells) pulling a sleigh, arrived at the door and out we ran. The morning was one of those never-to-be-forgotten ones. Cold, but everything sparkling like crystal as the landscape was covered with shimmering hoarfrost. The whole world sparkled and dazzled in crisp beauty as we skimmed along, the horses hoofs beating a rhythm in the crunchy snow. We were warm as toast as we snuggled together under blankets for the 1½ mile ride to Grandma's house.

I have such wonderful memories of many family gatherings, but Grandma's place for Christmas was a favorite. I recall with pleasure my fun with cousins, the abundance of good food, opening our gifts, and the music and singing that was always a big part of family gatherings. The ride home was a quieter one than the morning ride. We would peek out at the winter sky full of brilliant stars. From beneath our warm blankets we sighed with a mixture of deep contentment, happiness, and weariness. We would soon be home and fast asleep in our own warm beds.

There Was Always
Something to Do

A PICNIC EXCURSION

Maple Leaf Club, *Family Herald and Weekly Star*
August 12, 1901

Johnstone Willett (10)
Gore Bay, Ont.

One bright August morning last summer there was an excursion from this place to the north shore of Lake Huron, to hold a picnic at the little village of Cutler. Nearly three hundred people went on one small steamer, and had an enjoyable trip. The boat left Gore Bay, about nine o'clock, and after a pleasant little voyage we arrived at Cutler just as the mill whistle blew for dinner. Saw mills are very numerous along the north shore and we met several booms of logs that were being towed to the mills by pretty tugs. We had some difficulty in passing the booms and in one place our boat stopped to let a boom come down a narrow channel that we were passing through.

There was very pretty scenery along our route. Granite mountains rose on our left, and small islands were plentiful on our right. Some of these were used as summer resorts, and people were picking blueberries on some of the larger islands. On one rocky island we saw three tents arranged in the form of a triangle. The one nearest was red, the second was white, and the other one was blue. We saw several other tents, but none so pretty as the first three that we saw together.

Soon we reached the little village, and then the boat whistled, and we were not long in getting off the boat after she was at the moorings.

We went into a little grove, where we ate our dinner, and then went to see the mill. We saw them cutting timber, laths and shingles all at once.

We started home about six o'clock after having a good day's fun. When we came to this channel again the boom was there yet. The tug had been disabled so we had to go back and go through another channel. We overtook another steamer at Spanish River, and had a hot race for about thirty minutes when the other boat drew away from us. When the steamer passed many rushed over to see it, and nearly tipped our boat.

It was ten o'clock when we got home, and although tired and hungry, we felt that we had had a very enjoyable picnic excursion.

A BOB SLED

Maple Leaf Club, *Family Herald and Weekly Star*
December 6, 1911

Ernest Q. Heare (13)
Allan's Mills, Ont.

Dear Maple Leaves:

This is my second letter to your charming Club. It is about two months since I last wrote, but like many others failed to see it in print.

Well, I am going to tell you about a pair of sleighs I have that my brother made for me about three years ago.

He made three sleighs, two front ones and one hind one, and then he painted a pair of them. Every winter I go out with them and draw wood to the house.

I have a hand-sleigh, too, and I go back to a hill in our fields when the crust is hard, and when you go down you go away into the field.

A SCHOOL PICNIC

Maple Leaf Club, *Family Herald and Weekly Star*
August 2, 1911

Gladys M. Davidson (13)
North Grande Pre, N.S.

Now girls and boys, I suppose most of you have gone for a picnic in the woods. I have, so I am going to tell you about one I went to last summer.

All the boys and girls in our school, our teacher, and a few others, numbering in all about twenty-six, gathered at the schoolhouse at 1 p.m. with their baskets. When all had arrived, we started for a place known to us as "The Bluff," it was not very far, so we soon got there. The Bluff is a high bank and twice a day the water of the Minas Basin washes away the sand at the foot of it.

The 24th of May parade in Victoria, 1925 (BC Provincial Archives [82691]).

We found a cool place to put our baskets and then we sat down in the shade to rest and to eat candy.

After we had rested a while we played games such as "charades," "hide and go seek," etc. The boys had a game of football while the girls looked on. Then we had a nice game of baseball and by this time we were beginning to get hungry, so we sought out a nice shady place and the girls began to lay the table, which consisted of a tablecloth spread on the grass. When this was completed we all sat down on the grass around the table to have a feast of cakes, pies, doughnuts, cookies, tarts, sandwiches, and other things too numerous to mention. Then last and best of our feast came ice-cream and good ice-cream it was too. My! but it did taste good, especially on a hot day, and we had a nice piece of cake with it and it tasted lovely.

The girls cleared away the dishes and put them in the baskets. We left very little but the dishes and a few crumbs.

None of us felt much like playing any games now, so we strolled down to the seashore, the tide was out quite a distance, but a few who were not quite as tired as the rest walked down to the water's edge, while the rest sat down on the grass. By the time we got back from the water we were all pretty tired so we started for home. We reached there about dark, after having spent a very pleasant afternoon in the woods.

CHRISTMAS IN A PRISON CAMP

From *A Child in Prison Camp* ©1971 by Shizuye Takashima, published by Tundra Books.

The Takashima family was among those Japanese-Canadian families who, in 1942, were moved from the West Coast to prison camps in the interior of British Columbia. Shizuye's parents struggled to keep family ties and cultural roots strong.

Christmas at Home

I swing my legs to and fro, Japanese music fills our tiny room. Mrs. Kono has a small record player. From this black, leather box, with shining handles which we turn from time to time, glorious music comes. In the hot burning oven, our Christmas chicken is cooking. It sputters and makes funny noises. The lemon pies father baked are already on the table. He has been cooking all day. They look so nice, my favorite pies. Only father can bake such lovely tasty pies. He must put magic into them.

Father is an excellent cook. Before he became a gardener, he worked as a chef in a big restaurant and in hotels. And now, he still cooks on holidays or when we have many guests. I love watching him cook. He never uses a measuring cup, mostly his hands. He's always tasting, making gurgling, funny noises in his throat (for Japanese are allowed to make a lot of noise when they eat; especially when they drink tea or eat soup). Father closes his slanted eyes and tastes it, then he gives me a tiny bit. He and mother always treat me special, I guess because I'm the youngest and not as strong as Yuki. She doesn't mind: she knows I love her. I watch my father cook and I listen. The old song sounds full of joy.

— — —

Father ties a towel around his head. Mother hands him a bowl. He raises his arm, dances around. He is graceful as he waves his arm and bowl in time with the music. We all laugh. Mr. Kono joins him and sings. It is an old folk song.

Mother claps her hands in time with the rhythm. She is looking at my slippers, the ones David sent us for Christmas. She has a little smile. I know her thoughts are with David; this is the first Christmas he is not with us. We all sing. The music seems to grow louder. Little Kay-fo too joins us. We all sing. Yuki, the Konos and the whole room seems to fade. I see Japan. The snow is gone. I see happy rice planters with their bright kimonos, their black hair tied with printed towels, the gentle wind, with lovely Mount Fuji, Fuji-san itself, in the distance. The music, our voices, go beyond our house, out into the snow, past the mountains and into space, and this special day is made more magic, and I know I shall remember it forever.

CELEBRATING CHINESE NEW YEAR

From *West Coast Chinese Boy* ©1979 by Sing Lim,
published by Tundra Books.

*Sing Lim grew up in Vancouver's Chinatown during the early
1920s. Although life was often difficult and all members of the
family worked hard, Sing Lim recalls holidays and festivals as
happy times.*

To the average Chinese family like ours, Christmas was just
another day. Mr. Lam, still grateful to my father, sent a bottle of
liquor. That was the only thing that happened.

But to the Chinese peddlers, it was an important time. Many
Chinese peddled fish and vegetables to earn a living. Their
routes went all over Vancouver, spanning as much as five miles.
The peddlers were polite, dependable and honest, and well liked
by the white community. Just before Christmas they wrapped
little packages of candied ginger, lai-chee nuts or tea to give to
friends and customers. Many of them were in areas without
stores or regular transport and, for some, their Chinese peddler
was the only person to visit at Christmas with a little gift. To this
day, many white people of my generation remember those visits
with pleasure.

Although we didn't celebrate Christmas, we children we
were not too disappointed because the Chinese Lunar New Year
followed only a month of so later. Our mother dressed us up and
gave us haircuts. We were given "lucky money" (lai see) to buy
candy and firecrackers. We visited homes, stores and tong community centres where we could help ourselves to dried candied
sweets, water chestnuts, coconuts, lotus and red watermelon
seeds. They were set out in wooden boxes with eight containers,
all beautifully lacquered. Near the boxes were fruit, pastries and
a pot of tea in a rattan basket lined with cloth to keep it warm.

Back in the apartment mother was busy preparing the chicken
given us by Mr. Jake. He had a small pig and chicken farm outside
of town, and a few days before New Year's he gave us and other
families a live chicken. Mr. Jake appreciated our having saved
scraps of food throughout the year to use as slop for his pigs.

It was a happy occasion when it snowed around our New Year's, just as it is around Christmas time. It rains most of the winter in Vancouver, but I remember one year when everything was white. The color of our holiday seemed all the brighter. On the way home from school we built a real Chinese snowman with a colorful bib. The younger children flew their balloons, while one boy set off firecrackers.

OH! MY POOR DUCK

Reprinted with permission from Andy MacDonald, *Bread and Molasses* (Don Mills: Musson Press, 1976).

Andy MacDonald, son of a Cape Breton coal miner, was one of twelve children. The family survived the 1930s on his father's meagre salary, his mother's saving ways, and whatever the children managed to make.

That feeling of Christmas for a child is one he'll never have again. Just to hear the word "Christmas" spoken was a thrill, even in July.

A week before Christmas we were at our best, willing to do anything for any member of the family without argument. A few days before Christmas, Pa would give each of us a dollar bill to buy something for ourselves. How we appreciated that! What great affection we had for Pa who had been so rough on us throughout the year.

Billy was the slickest of us all. He would always buy Pa a good substantial present, not with thoughts of love, but speculating on a gift from Pa that would cost more than his. With the Christmas spirit spreading over us, we'd go to town next day to look over the toys.

Our scheme was to buy as many gifts as a dollar could buy, without taking too much out of the dollar. I bought a metal duck with a winder on it. When wound the duck would flap and quack. It cost sixty-nine cents, but for the first few days it was priceless. As soon as I'd open my eyes in the morning, the duck would be on my mind. I guess I thought too much of it. The greatness of it couldn't go on forever. One morning Teedy walked on it with a pair of heavy boots and cut off all circulation to the quack and the flap. We tried everything to repair it. I can still see the look on the duck's face, as though it were suffering pains and aches in its crushed tin body.

> [Teedy had a frog that croaked and jumped when it was wound up. Teedy issued an order that he would wind the frog twice to my once.]

Then one mild day in January when Teedy was nowhere in sight and snow was scarce, I figured the frog would do better outside in the wide open spaces. So I took Mr. Frog outside for his first outdoor show.

> [At this point the coal man came with his horse and cart.]

I had to open the gate for him and his horse. Seeing the horse was a real novelty: I forgot about the frog and concentrated on the live horse, watching the way he knew where to go and what to do automatically. The coal was dumped and the horse took his round-about course to turn. I watched spellbound by the sight of his muscular rump, while those big cart wheels, spoke by spoke, went over Teedy's frog. In seconds the frog was completely round.

> [Teedy was devastated, so his brothers pooled their eighty-two cents and bought two live rabbits. They took them home, and put them in the old hen house. Alas, a board fell and killed one of them.]

We gave him [rabbit] a burial Pope Paul would have received. We prayed at his funeral, placed him in a box, and marched him to a special place in the garden. Ashes to ashes and dust to dust were sprinkled, and the lid softly closed over him.

SPACE, FREEDOM, ACTIVE, LOVE

Ian and Lee Rennie share their memories of sunny Winnipeg.

As Lee and I talk about Winnipeg childhoods in the '30s, there are certain expressive words that come to mind, such as space, freedom, active, love—words which need to be fleshed out. And of course, whatever some may think, Winnipeg was hardly the boondocks in those days; in fact, it was the third largest city in Canada.

Space meant lots of room—even in the cities: rivers and riverbanks, creeks and gullies, large parks—Assiniboine, Polo Park, Kildonan—to name a few. With just a brief walk, and over a trestle, you were right out in the country, where you sensed the infinite horizon and the glorious clouds.

"Color-color." Keith and Kim Gosse, 1952.

Freedom began as soon as school was out. In five to five and a half months of winter (November to mid-April) it meant tobogganing down river banks and gulleys, and at a party down the great slides at Polo Park, skating—at local skating rinks and on the river, and as one grew older, skiing. These late afternoons finished at supper time. In the warm weather there was bicycle riding, which in the summer holidays could go on all day and right into the evening. And the weather always seems to be good – good and cold, good and hot, and just plain good. Seldom did days ever seem to be spoiled by rain, so there always seemed to be the freedom to do what you wished.

Active seems to encapsulate one of the qualities of life. Life was always busy, usually at your own instigation or that of your friends. Time didn't seem to hang on your hands.

Love was always present. As a child you were not particularly reflective about it – you just took it for granted. Yet now as you look back, and realize how difficult the Dirty Thirties on the prairies were for our parents, we are amazed at the strength of character that they exhibited. My father was in the grain business, in the Winnipeg office of the Saskatchewan Wheat Pool, yet often his stories were of how much worse off were the farmers. Lee's father began to develop serious arthritis of the spine, until as a relatively young man he was virtually doubled over. Yet we were given constant love, with little or no idea of what our parents were suffering in worry and apprehension.

As we look back we thank God that we were privileged to be prairie kids.

VICTORIA DAY IN PONOKA

Holidays were important events because there was often a celebration or at least a break from the daily routine. Lis Schmidt Robert shares her memory of a very special event.

I can't recall full details from my 6th year of life, but that year our Victoria Day celebration went something like this: We had all received small Union Jacks at school. Then ten or so children in our neighbourhood decided it would be a good idea to put on a parade. We put our family's cylinder record player in our wagon, put on the record "Rule Britannia" or "There'll Always Be an England" (I don't remember which) and turned on the player. We then marched around the block pulling the wagon, singing with the record, and waving our flags.

I find it interesting to look back on that event. Mom and Dad were new immigrants from Denmark and I don't think the British sentiment meant anything to them and probably not to us either. But I recall this event with both pleasure and amusement.

A LOT OF STRENUOUS OUTDOOR FUN

Norman St. Clair-Sulis recalls his Nova Scotia childhood.

Most of our activities were seasonal and all outside. (I lived with my grandparents who raised me and my two sisters as my mother had died in childbirth.) The tides came into the basin from the Bay of Fundy. It was called a basin rather than a bay, because so much water rushed in with the incoming tide. There was a similar rush in the opposite direction when the tide fell. It was referred to as filling and emptying the basin.

Spring

When the leaves were just forming on the poplar and birch trees my cousin and I and other boys would climb as high as possible until the trees would bend over. The object of the game was to see who could go the greatest distance without touching the ground. When the tree bent over you had to jump or grab another tree. Sometimes you would take a nasty fall or get very scratched from striking the branches. This was always a lot of fun, but it was rather strenuous.

Summer

In late June the ocean was warm enough for swimming. We would walk out on the mud flats to the water's edge, nearly a mile, and wait for the tide to turn. At this point the mud was very slippery and deep. We liked to run and slide in the mud. If you fell there was little chance of injury, just a scrape now and then. We, boys and girls, had wonderful mud fights. As the water began to come in we would wash off. The water heated up as it came in over the flats.

Occasionally we dug clams with our fingers. When the tide was coming in the clams were near the surface and squirted water. We would run to the spot were the clam squirted and quickly dig. We washed off the clams and cooked them later on an old oven grate placed on a circle of rocks. The clams were covered with seaweed and steamed over the fire. When the clams were cooked the shells popped open. In the late 1940s we were not concerned with pollution. Now I understand no one can eat the clams.

Fall

My grandfather died when I was 10 in 1949. He gave me his father's shotgun. He and my father taught me how to use it. I fell on my butt the first time I fired it. It was a double barrel shotgun. It had a very long barrel and it was not easy for me to carry it around. My cousin and I used to hunt grouse and pheasants. I was not the best of shots and the gun was heavy. Shells were rationed, so we often just scared out the birds and tried to see who could find the most in the short daylight hours after school. My grandmother did not want me to have the gun; however, grandfather prevailed as he was very ill with cancer.

Winter

How can I forget Sunset Hill. Those high hills passed for mountains where I grew up. We had an ancient but well-built toboggan and wooden bobsled. Neighbours used oxen or horses. The bobsled was not easy to steer and there were many accidents. More than one boy or girl ended up with a broken arm. The summit of Sunset hill was reached via a winding gravel road, which in winter was not used by motor cars. The road became covered with ice because the snow often melted and froze again. The bobsled on its descent seemed to us to reach a great speed. Sometimes we had to run it up on the snow bank in order to slow down. It was a challenge to make the bends in the road without crashing into someone coming up the hill or going down in a regular sled.

I enjoyed recalling these happy times. If you had not asked, they would have remained tucked away. Thank you!

FUN WAS SEASONAL IN EDMONTON

W.J. (Bud) Phillips and his friends knew how to have fun through all seasons of the year.

Fun was seasonal in Edmonton. As the skies and the ground conditions changed, so did our methods for assuring laughter, seeking adventure, and creating the stories that made the fun last.

Summer

In June and July, all around town, in sheds and garages, in back yards and empty lots we built our soapboxes in preparation for the race on the first weekend of August. A soapbox was a work of art. The more it could resemble the flashy race cars of the day, the more impressed the crowd would be as it whooshed past on the day of the Derby. It had to have four wheels and the front wheels had to be able to turn so that you could navigate the long downward journey from the MacDonald Hotel, down the McDougall Hill to the flats at the bottom.

Now a soapbox was not only a vehicle for show. It had to have speed and agility and it had to be constructed to endure. That's where most of us found the challenge. There were theories. Every year the theories changed. Would bigger wheels at the back make the thing go faster downhill? If the driver sat nearer the front would the balance be better? Would it be better to have the wheels farther apart? Or closer?

On the day of the derby they closed the road down McDougall Hill and the crowds lined the hillside for nearly half a mile. All afternoon the waves of sleek—and not so sleek—soapboxes came down the hill at wildly different speeds and with varying degrees of agility and endurance. For some the race ended at the first curve. Others came to sudden stops along the curb. For some it ended before it began when one of the wheels fell off as the thing was being pushed to the starting line. For others the long ride down the hill, with the wind in your face and the crowd cheering you on was the most exhilarating thing all year. And for everyone who had worked for weeks planning, conceiving, designing, and building the vehicle, there was always next year.

Fall

Back to school meant back with your friends on the team. We followed the Pro teams so in the fall we played baseball and imagined ourselves in the world series. Later in the fall we prepared ourselves for our version of the Grey Cup game — ours was played on the morning of the day of the big game. And all winter long we mimicked and learned from the Edmonton Flyers and got to go to the games with our dad — or maybe our friend's dad. Ken McCauley and Pug Young, Gordie Watts, and Elmer Kreller were my heroes. It was absolutely the very best when we beat the Calgary Stampeders. Every Saturday night we would play Monopoly and listen to Hockey Night in Canada. I realize now it didn't matter if the Leafs won or lost. We were inspired to play street hockey the next day or practised all the harder on the open frozen rink down near the school where we were preparing for our big chance some day.

Winter

Then there were the toboggans and bobsleighs. We played on them with such determination and vigour that it became dangerous. I remember wrapping Bobby Cushley around a tree trunk at the bottom of Deadman's Hill in Whitemud because our bobsled didn't turn when it was supposed to. I remember riding a toboggan right through a thick bush because the four of us on it couldn't get it to stop or turn, and we didn't have the sense to fall off it on purpose and hold the rope. I remember trying to find just the right wax for the bottom of the toboggan so that ours would surely pass all the others on the open race down the hill under the ski jump. And I remember thinking that it must be wonderful to sweep down the snow-covered wooden track on the high ski jump and take off through the air on skis, and see the skyline of the city from up there. But I never tried it.

Spring

When the snow melted in March or April there were at least three weeks of great matchstick racing. You and somebody else could put your matchstick in the water along the curb and walk a block following the hazards of its journey to the manhole at

the end of the block. The races were like miniature marathons —
here a rock or a clump of leaves, there a stretch of fast water,
here a curve because of a frozen block of ice, there a little water-
fall over a branch or stone. We ran home at noon to rush
through lunch so that we could race our matchsticks all the way
to school. That was the direction of the flow of runoff water in
our neighbourhood. The first matchstick down the manhole
won the race, but the trouble was then you lost the winning
matchstick and had to get another one for the next race. Later,
when we changed houses and schools, we raced home at noon
because the water ran toward our house in that neighbourhood.
I know that for certain because a couple of years we had floods
in our basement.

All Year Long

There were some other things that came to mind when I started
to think about what we did for fun in my childhood. Most of my
friends and I had paper routes as soon as we were old enough to
get one. I was 12 when I got my first one. And the *Edmonton Journal* required that we cash in on Saturday morning at the Journal
building. So every Friday evening we would have to go around
our route to be sure everyone had paid for the week of papers.
And every Saturday morning for at least three years I took the
bus to the bottom of MacDougall Hill, got off at the bottom with
at least a dozen friends, and ran up the 122 stairs that were the
alternative way to get up the escarpment. It was a test of
endurance, but looking back it was probably a good time to
build up our lung capacity and strengthen our heart muscles.
There was a routine on Saturday morning. After cashing in we
got on the bus and went to the Garneau Theatre for the morning
matinees and the "good deed club." We got to follow the serials
of Hopalong Cassidy, Superman, Zorro, and Roy Rogers, and
there were prizes and cartoons, and lots of popcorn.

One of my fondest memories was the Sunday afternoons at the
home of our Sunday school teacher who also had the longest, most
complex, and neatest electric train set-up I could imagine. It took
up the whole attic of his house and once a month after church the
Sunday school class went to Bill's house where his parents had

prepared hot dogs and we played with the train for hours. We built things out of balsa wood for the "village" in the attic—log houses, tents, little cars and trucks, a mountain or two—and we imagined great journeys, discussed important things, and found a safe place to share our hopes, our dreams, and even our questions.

ACROSS THE PRAIRIES ON A PONY

Maple Leaf Club, *Family Herald and Weekly Star*
December 6, 1911

RURAL
Alta.
(I hope you are all better by now, Rural, and that your trip to Ontario will make you strong for good and all. — Ed.)

Dear Maple Leaves:

I live in Alberta and like it fine. I don't know what I would ever do without the coulees, the wild flowers, the wild berries, and the wild and free prairie.

I am never happier than when I am on horseback striking across the prairie. I have a roan pony, and I think so much of her that I don't know what I would do without her.

I am a great reader and read everything I can get hold of. I have read by Cooper, "The Pioneer," "The Deerslayer," and "The Pathfinder." I have read "Bleak House," by Dickens. Also "Uncle Tom's Cabin," "Ten Nights in a Bar," "Tom Brown at Oxford," "Ivanhoe," and many others, besides all the serials in the Family Herald for about four years.

I have been sick for over three weeks, but I am getting a little better now. Please excuse bad writing as my hand is pretty shaky. I am going to Ontario this winter for my health, as this country is too high for me.

Well, I guess I had better leave off, as this is getting to be quite a long letter.

MY FAVOURITE PASTIME WAS
GOING TROUTING

*Nick Green grew up in Winterton, a fishing village located
on the east coast of Newfoundland.*

Everyone was involved in fishing. My favourite pastime was
going trouting. Now in Newfoundland when you say you are
going fishing, that means you were going for codfish. Everything else you named, like trouting meant you went for trout.
My mom tied a safety pin to my line, but I think my father took
pity on me and tied on a barbed hook. For trouting, you had to
have a bamboo pole, which cost 25 cents, and a float. I got a piece
of cork out of a bottle, and I drilled a hole in it and blackened it
and made my own float. Fish hooks you had to buy, and in those
days I suppose you could buy them for less than a penny each.
Trout could be caught in the brook which ran right by our house,
or in ponds, and there were several within an hour's walk.

We were always in boats because we grew up with them.
We'd take the rowboats and go out and try to catch lobster —
never venturing too far from the shore. I remember once we got
out aways, and my uncle was coming in and saw us. He came
over and said, "Have fun, boys. Work hard," meaning "You got
here, you can get home." But he kept an eye on us to make sure
we got back.

Another thing we did on a cold winter day was galleying or
galley-gigging — jumping from one ice pan to another. It was a very
dangerous thing to do. I was forbidden to do it, but you know
what it is when you get in with guys. We did it in ponds where the
water was not deep, but it was a deadly game in deep water.

And, of course, I was always building little sailboats and sailing them in the brook. I made them of board or wood and I cut
sails from pieces of cloth. They were crudely made, as I sewed
them myself. We raced them on the ponds. The girls didn't make
boats much, or go trouting as much, but they played tiddley as
much as the boys.

Our games were self-organized. We'd get together, agree to a
game, and that would get us started. Our games didn't require
much equipment. For tiddley, the only things you needed were

sticks and rocks, and those were readily available. You took a saw and cut a tree to the size you wanted. Tiddley was played with a stick about twelve inches long, another about three feet long, and some stones. Both boys and girls played that game.

In winter, it was mainly sledding. There was a series of three hills, I guess about a mile long. We'd get five or six sleds going with several children on each sled. There was very little skating. I owned skates, but there weren't any facilities for skating. Some years the ponds (as we called them) froze over early and there might be a bit of skating, but normally the ice was pretty rough and covered with snow. The coldest temperature I can remember was −3°F. You could have lots of snowball fights because the snow was generally pretty soft most of the time.

We played ball with sponge balls. If the ball was caught before it hit the ground, you were out. If someone threw the ball and hit you before you got to the base you were out. Another game we played, especially in the spring, was buttons. It was similar to playing marbles. You put a little peg in the ground and you pitched buttons. Whoever got closest to the peg would flip the button and call odd or even or whatever it was. If you lost, your buttons went to whoever was the lucky caller or whoever put them closer to the peg. We could entertain ourselves. I don't know what the kids do these days.

There was a lot of socializing among people. You didn't wait to be asked to go, you just went. There were certain places where people gathered and if it wasn't too cold you'd see the men gathered somewhere around the wharf. There was more chatting and yarning. Yarning is the word that comes to my mind; that's what we call it in Newfoundland. I think that is probably the most descriptive word. Seafaring people are usually very superstitious and I'd go and listen of some of their yarns and I'd be almost scared to go home. Later I'd lie in bed almost shaking.

In Winterton, each church had a school, the Anglican School and the United Church School had two rooms, and the the Salvation Army School had one room, with kids from grades 1 to grade 11. I learned a lot about Shakespeare when I was supposed to be doing my arithmetic. The play being studied might be in grade 11, and I might be in grade 6, but I listened anyway.

Each church had a Christmas concert. We went dressed in our best—we had one suit—usually a well-worn serge for the men. There were few gifts as there was very little money. I recall a second-hand sled I got. We had those little cap pistols. You could buy brown strips of paper with little brown dots of powder on them.

At Christmas the Orangemen and the Fisherman (that was the Orange Lodge and the Society of United Fishermen) would have a parade. People would get out their muzzle-loading guns and put a charge of powder in them so they'd have a 21-gun salute as the parade went by. I still have my grandfather's muzzle loader. The brand name is Towers, as it was assembled in the Tower of London. Another quaint thing we did at Christmas was mummering, mostly as teenagers. You would always go out as a group.

I didn't get a gun until I was 15, because during the war you couldn't buy a gun, but the minute the war was over I got a gun. We were used to being outside and boys were pretty careful with guns. There are no wolves in Newfoundland unless they've imported them in recent years. And there were no squirrels and no snakes, although I believe squirrels have been imported recently.

Those days, all the codfish was salted and dried so there was drying flakes all over the place. We had quite a few chores, hauling in and cutting up the firewood. We had no running water so we had to carry in water. I helped with haying, which meant that during the summer I had to miss my favourite radio programs—*Tarzan* and *Superman*, as well as *Pepper Young's Family* and *Lucy Linton's Stories from Life*. From the time I was thirteen we had what I called "chicken every Sunday." Every Saturday I had to catch the chicken, cut the head off, clean it, and pluck it. I used to hate that job. And the chicken had better be plucked properly, or I was in trouble.

My brothers and sisters were fairly musical. We had an old-fashioned organ and had many singsongs around it. We played Chinese Checkers, regular checkers, but no cards. Dad viewed playing cards as a sin, so we didn't play cards. I think I read every book in the little settlement, including *Pilgrim's Progress*. I read everything I could get my hands on. People all around knew I was a reader and if they had a book they'd bring it to me. Our only newspaper was the weekly *Family Herald*. I read it from cover to cover. Initially, Dad used to read it aloud. That would be some of our entertainment. When we finished with it, it went to the outhouse as a substitute for toilet paper. I hated Eaton's catalogue, but the *Family Herald* wasn't bad.

Church picnics were mainly for the Sunday school—there would be three-legged races and sack races. Everybody came to the picnic. There were no hot dogs, hamburgers, or ice cream. At a birthday party you would be served a piece of bread and jelly—that would be your treat.

My most pleasant memory is probably the first time my grandfather took me fishing in his rowboat with its removable mast and sail. I had several wonderful fishing trips with him. (My grandfather died just before my eighth birthday.) But I could probably come up with ten or eleven things like that and still would wonder which is my most pleasant memory. I remember going on several picnics with Mom and Dad. People didn't do that very often, but every now and then we'd go off—just the family. We'd have roast "Tomcod," a small cod (main bone, sound bone not removed as in the split fish) salted and dried. We would wrap it in paper, moisten it, and put it among the coals. We would toast homemade bread over the coals of the fire (no baker's bread available then) and, of course, have a cup of tea.

A VERY SPECIAL TIME

As the Palmer family of Freeland, Prince Edward Island, had no sons, Donna Palmer Ebbutt and the two sisters nearest her age did much of the farm work. But, as Donna recalls, there was always time for fun and to celebrate holidays and special events.

After the apples were picked and the potatoes and mangels dug, sorted, and stored, then came Halloween. We didn't have many outfits but we went out trick or treating on Halloween night. We usually got an apple but no candy. Some of the young guys went around upsetting outdoor toilets or taking gates off their hinges and then we couldn't find our gates. We didn't upset toilets, we just screamed and howled and made a bit of noise. It was a real fun night for us.

Christmas was a very special time. We always had Christmas concerts in the school. I remember one year when my oldest sister was principal of a school, she bought the three of us dresses — 99 cents each — so we would be all dressed up for the Christmas concert because we all had a part in a dialogue or singing. I remember there were candles on the tree in the hall because there was no electricity.

We always cut our own Christmas tree. We'd take the sleigh and go out to the back of our field to cut our tree. Then we three kids would haul it home and put it up in the parlor — as it was called then — and Dad would sit and watch us and smoke his pipe. We'd put the tree in a bucket of potatoes and then we would take binder twine and hook it to each side of the bay window so it wouldn't fall over. All we had for decorations were those red and green streamers, cranberries we strung, and some tinfoil icicles. Actually it always turned out to be a nice tree and every year my Dad said it was the best tree we ever had.

Christmas Eve we always went to midnight service at the Anglican Church. There would be snow on the ground glistening in the moonshine. Dad used to put us in the wood sleigh and cover us with a buffalo [robe]. As we were on our way up to the church we could see the line of horses and sleighs and hear their [harness] bells ringing as they came to the church. Everybody had bells on their horses that night. And when we got in and around the fire, everyone was so happy because it was warm and cozy and because it was Christmas Eve. It was a night to behold. Mum stayed home to prepare a big dinner because we always had the minister and his wife stay overnight after the service. We'd come home and Mum would have the table all set and we'd have roast duck and potatoes and turnips and plum pudding.

Christmas morning was a big morning. We'd run down stairs about 4 o'clock in the morning to see our socks and then hop into bed with Mum and Dad. We did not have that many gifts. From Santa Claus we usually got an apple and an orange, some nuts, and that hard candy with the streaks in it. Then one year my two older sisters hung up pillowcases and my Dad filled then full of turnips and that was the end of that. We were so excited about the few things we had in our sock, but it made our Christmas. I always wanted to be a nurse when I grew up and my parents always managed to find a nurse doll to stick in my sock. The dolls were made out of a kind of sawdust and filled with a kind of straw. I think they cost 25 cents.

We had an aunt and uncle who were quite well off, and they always saw that we had a nice fresh brand-new nightie for Christmas, and that was a highlight — to crawl into a nice new nightie. Another uncle, who was a dentist, and his wife used to give each of us a new dress or a pair of mitts with 25 cents in the thumb. I remember one Christmas getting a tea set and all Christmas Day we played we were serving tea.

As far as Christmas at home — it was a really joyful time. Christmas dinner was with all Dad's brothers and sisters. My sister played the organ and we'd gather around and sing all kinds of Christmas hymns and songs. So we would look our best, we'd curl our hair. We used to wrap our hair around strips of brown paper. When we took out the brown papers, our hair was curly.

School would go in again in January. Dad could not wait for a day when it stormed and the teacher would not be at school (and we had quite a few of those days on PEI) and we could play cards all day. A lot of the kids came to our place to play cards as well. Dad loved to play cards with us and Mum would see we were well fed with doughnuts and hot chocolate. We played with cut-outs from Sears catalogue, or maybe it was Eaton's catalogue. We drew and colored a lot, we played X's and 0's, I Spy, Hang the Man, and a lot of games such as Crokinole and Chinese Checkers. We helped Mum quilt and hook rugs. In fact, we were quilting and hooking at an early age but we thought this was all fun, and it was.

We took our hand and bob sleighs over to a nearby big hill. Three or four of us would get on the sleigh, go down the hill, and slide right across the frozen river. We also skated on the river, lit bonfires, and brought food to eat. All the kids from school came there to skate.

Valentine's Day was also a special day at school. We made our own valentines, cut out with scissors in the shape of a heart. I think I could still do that, you know. We'd color them and we'd always put a verse in them. "Roses are red, Violets are blue, Sugar is sweet, And so are you." That's the one I remember. And we got valentines from everybody. The teacher would have a box up at the front and you put your valentines in. Then she'd call out the names of who the valentines were sent to.

Adele, Florence, and Marion Newberry reading together, undated (Prince Edward Island Public Archives and Records Office [38885/66]).

Our parlor was at the end of a long hallway. Sometimes we decided to have a church service. We'd go upstairs where my Mum and my Grandma had lots of old hats. We'd put on a hat and get dressed up with some beads and put other things on and then come down. I played the organ. The neighbours' children were there too, and we'd go into the parlor all dressed up and sit down and a have a church service. And then one of my sisters would read from the Bible or make out she was reading from the Bible. Then we'd say "Amen." It was so much fun. I remember my childhood as a special, special time. We had to get out and make our own fun so we started early — and we had such a good time.

BIBLIOGRAPHY

Bell, Betty. *The Fair Land*. Victoria: Sono Nis Press, 1982.

Blashill, Lorraine. *Remembering the '50s*. Victoria: Orca, 1997.

Bliss, Jacqueline. "Seamless Lives: Pioneer Women of Saskatoon, 1883-1903." *Saskatchewan History* 43 (Aug. 1992): 90-91

Bouchard, David. Images by Henry Ripplinger. *"If You're Not from the Prairies...."* Vancouver: Raincoast Books, 1993.

Bourgeon, Nan. *Rubber Boots Are for Dancing*. Cloverdale: D.W. Friesen, 1979.

Broadfoot, Barry. *Next Year Country: Voices of Prairie People*. Toronto: McClelland & Stewart, 1988.

_____. *The Pioneer Years: Memories of Settlers Who Opened the West*. Markham: Paperjacks, 1978.

Browne, Jean. "Junior Red Cross." Papers and Proceedings of the Conference on Child Welfare, 1923.

Buchanan, Carl. "A Wintery Day on the Homestead" *The Beaver* 30, 2 (1976): 6-9.

Bullen, John. "Hidden Workers: Child Labour and the Household Economy in Early Industrial Ontario." *Labour/Le Travail* 18 (Fall 1986): 163-78.

Caswell, Maryanne. *Pioneer Girl*. Toronto: McGraw Hill, 1964.

Choy, Wayson. *Paper Shadows: A Chinatown Childhood*. Toronto: Viking, 1999.

Cochrane, Jean. *Down on the Farm: Childhood Memories of Farming in Canada*. Calgary: Fifth House, 1996.

Cochrane, Jean. *The One-Room School in Canada*. Markham: Fitzhenry and Whiteside, 1981.

Coleman, MacDonald. *Once Upon a Summer*. Red Deer: Kingfisher Press, 1978.

Collins, Robert. *Butter Down the Well: Reflections of a Canadian Childhood.* Vancouver: Douglas and McIntyre, 1980.

Copp, Terry. *The Anatomy of Poverty: The Condition of the Working Class in Montreal, 1897-1929.* Toronto: McClelland and Stewart, 1974.

Dow, Gwyn, and June Factor. *Australian Childhood: An Anthology.* South Yarra: McPhee and Gribble, 1991.

Downs, Robert Bingham. *Friedrich Froebel.* New York: G.K. Hall, 1978.

Dryden, Ken. "Soul on Ice: A Century of Canadian Hockey." *The Beaver* 80 (Dec. 2000-Jan. 2001): 1-23.

Eddington, Bryan. "Little Brother." *The Beaver* 80 (Oct-Nov 2000): 9-14.

Ellis, Sarah. *A Prairie as Wide as the Sea: The Immigrant Diary of Ivy Weatherall.* Toronto: Scholastic, 2002.

Fowke, Edith. *Red Rover, Red Rover: Children's Games Played in Canada.* Toronto: Doubleday, 1988.

_____. *Ring Around the Moon.* Toronto: McClelland and Stewart, 1988.

_____. *Sally Go Round the Sun.* New York: Doubleday, 1969.

Froebel, Friedrich. *The Education of Man.* New York: Appleton, 1909.

Gray, James. *The Boy from Winnipeg.* Toronto: Macmillan, 1970.

Gryski, Camilla, with images by Dusan Petricic. *Let's Play: Traditional Games of Childhood.* Toronto: Kids Can, 1995.

Haig-Brown, Celia. *Resistance and Renewal: Surviving the Indian Residential School.* Vancouver: Tillicum, 1989.

Harris, E.A. *Spokeshute: Skeena River Memories.* Victoria: Orca, 1990.

Howell, David, and Peter Lindsay. "Social Gospel and the Young Boy Problem." *Canadian Journal of the History of Sports* 17 (May 1986): 75-87.

Johnston, Basil. *Indian School Days.* Toronto: Key Porter, 1988.

Jones, David C. "'There Is Some Power about the Land' — The Western Agrarian Press and Country Ideology." *Journal of Canadian Studies/ Revue d'etudes canadiens* 17, 3 (Autumn 1982): 96-108.

Kelcey, Barbara E. "The Great Gopher War." *The Beaver* 79 (June-July 1999): 16-24.

Kelman, Suanne. "Redefining Family." *The Beaver* 80, 1 (Feb.-Mar. 2000): 44-54.

Kogawa, Joy. *Obasan.* Toronto: Lester and Orpen Dennys, 1961.

Krepps, Rex G. *As Sparks Fly Upward.* Cloverdale: D.W. Friesen, 1989.

The League of the Empire — An Imperial Union of Schools' and Pupils' Correspondence, 1922. Ontario Archives. RG2 P3.

Lewis, Norah L. "'Isn't This a Terrible War?': The Attitude of Children to Two World Wars." *Historical Studies in Education/Revue d' l'education* 7 (Fall 1995): 193-215.

_____. *I Want to Join Your Club: Letters from Rural Children, 1900-1920*. Waterloo: Wilfrid Laurier University Press, 1996.

Leyshon, Glynn A. "The Art of Play: Street Games In the Depression." *The Beaver* 79 (Aug.-Sept. 1999): 32-36.

Little, Jean. *Orphan at My Door: The Home Child Diary of Victoria Cope*. Toronto: Scholastic, 2001.

Marr, M. Lucille. "Church Teen Clubs, Feminized Organization? Tuxis Boys, Trail Rangers, and Canadian Girls in Training, 1919-1939." *Historical Studies in Education/Revue d'histoire de l'education* 3, 2 (Fall 1991): 249-67.

MacDonald, Andy. *Bread and Molasses*. Don Mills: Musson Press, 1976.

Magna Carta Day: A Sign Post Raised by English Speaking Nations on the Path of Civilization to World Peace. 1937. Violet McNaughton Papers. Saskatchewan Archives Board. A1 File 89.

McLean, Stuart. *When We Were Young: A Collection of Canadian Stories Selected and Introduced by Stuart McLean*. Toronto: Viking, 1996.

Mitchell, W.O. *Who Has Seen the Wind*. Toronto: Macmillian, 1947.

Morton, Desmond. "The Cadet Movement in Canada in the Moment of Canadian Militarism." *Journal of Canadian Studies* 13 (Summer 1979): 56-68.

Murray, Hilda Chaulk. *More than Fifty Percent: Woman's Life in a Newfoundland Outport*. St. John's: Breakwater, 1997.

O'Brien, Olive. *Running with the Wind*. Fernwood: Harrison, 1977.

Ontario Department of Education. "Summer School for Teachers at the Ontario Agricultural College, Guelph, 1909." Ontario Archives, Toronto, RG 2 Series.

Opie, Iona, and Peter Opie. *Lore and Language of Schoolchildren*. Oxford: Clarendon, 1951.

Parker, Margaret. "Behind the Sateen Curtain." In Hugh A. Dempsey, ed. *Christmas in the West*. Saskatoon: Western Producer, 1982, pp. 141-44.

Porter, Helen. *Below the Bridge*. St. John's: Breakwater, 1979.

Powell, Ben W. *Labrador By Choice*. St. John's: Jesperson, 1979.

Prang, Margaret. "'The Girl God Would Have Me Be': The Canadian Girls in Training, 1915-1939." *Canadian Historical Review* 66 (1985): 154-84.

Ritchie, Charles. *My Grandfather's House: Scenes of Childhood and Youth*. Toronto: Macmillan, 1987.

Saunders, Gary L. *Rattles and Steadies: The Memories of a Gander River Man*. St. John's: Breakwater, 1986.

Sharpe, Christopher A. "The 'Race of Honour': An Analysis of Enlistments and Casualties in the Armed Forces of Newfoundland: 1914-1918." *Newfoundland Studies* 4, 1 (1988): 27-55.

Sherwood, Herbert Francis. "Children of the Land: The Story of the MacDonald Movement in Canada." Reprinted with permission from *The Outlook*, New York, April 23, 1910. Ontario Archives, Toronto. Pamphlet #266, 1910.

Silverman, Eliane Leslau. *The Last Best West: Women on the Alberta Frontier, 1890-1930*. Montreal: Eden Press, 1984.

Sing Lim, *West Coast Chinese Boy*. Montreal: Tundra Books, 1979.

Sisson, Hal C., and Dwayne D. Rowe. *Coots, Codgers and Curmudgeons: Things Were More Like They Used to Be Then than They Are Now*. Victoria: Orca, 1994.

Soeur Marie Ursula. *Civilisation traditionelle des Lavalois*. Quebec: Les Presses de l'Université Laval, 1951.

Sterling, Shirley. *My Name Is Seepeetza*. Vancouver: Groundwood Books, 1982.

Sutherland, Neil. *Children in English-Canadian Society: Framing the Twentieth-Century Consensus*. Waterloo: Wilfrid Laurier University Press, 2000.

_____. *Growing Up: Childhood in English Canada from the Great War to the Age of Television*. Toronto: University of Toronto Press, 1997.

_____. "'I Can't Recall When I Didn't Help': The Working Lives of Pioneering in Twentieth-Century British Columbia." *Social History/ Histoire sociale* 24 (Nov. 1991): 267-88.

_____. "'We Always Had Things to Do': Paid and Unpaid Work of Anglophone Children between the 1920s and the 1960s." *Labour/Le travail* 25 (Spring 1990): 105-41.

Symons R.D. *Grandfather Symons' Homestead Book*. Saskatoon: Western Producer Books, 1981.

Takashima, Shizuye. *A Child in a Prison Camp*. Montreal: Tundra Books, 1971.

Turner, Nancy J. *Plant Technology of First Peoples of British Columbia*. Vancouver: University of British Columbia, 1989.

West, Elliott. *Growing Up with the Country: Childhood on the Western Frontier*. Albuquerque: University of New Mexico Press, 1989.

White, Howard. *Spilsbury's Coast*. Madeira Park: Harbour Publishing, 1988.

Young, Alan R. "'We Throw the Torch': Canadian Memorials of the Great War and the Mythology of Heroic Sacrifice." *Journal of Canadian Studies* 14 (Winter 1989-90): 5-29